THE BRECHT MEMOIR

DEMCO

Also by Eric Bentley
from Northwestern University Press

The Pirandello Commentaries
Rallying Cries: Three Plays
Thinking about the Playwright

Northwestern is also the publisher of
Pirandello's Major Plays
(English versions by Eric Bentley)

THE BRECHT MEMOIR

Eric Bentley

WITH A FOREWORD BY MARTIN ESSLIN

Northwestern University Press
Evanston, Illinois

Northwestern University Press
Evanston, Illinois 60201

An earlier version of this work appeared in *Theater*, Spring 1983, as
"The Brecht Memoir." The postscript was first published in *Delos*,
Winter 1988-89, as "The Eric Bentley Memoir: A Postscript." *The
Brecht Memoir* first published by PAJ Publications, 1985. New edition
published in Great Britain by Carcanet Press Ltd., 1989. Northwestern
University Press edition published 1991 by arrangement with Carcanet
Press Ltd.

96 95 94 93 92 91   6 5 4 3 2 1

Library of Congress Cataloging-in-Publication Data

Bentley, Eric, 1916–
    The Brecht memoir / Eric Bentley ; with a foreword by Martin
Esslin.
        p.   cm.
    Reprint. Originally published: London : Carcanet Press, 1989.
    Includes index.
    ISBN 0-8101-0916-6 (alk. paper)   — ISBN 0-8101-0917-4
(pbk. : alk. paper)
        1. Brecht, Bertolt, 1898–1956. 2. Authors, German—20th century—
Biography.   I. Title.
PT2603.R397Z5594   1990
832'.912—dc20
[B]   90-21973
                                                                    CIP

The paper used in this publication meets the minimum requirements of
American National Standard for Information Sciences—Permanence of
Paper for Printed Library Materials, ANSI Z39.48-1984

DEDICATED TO THE MEMORY OF RUTH BERLAU (1906–74)

Lykken mellem to mennesker
er som den dunkle nat,
stille, men med de tusinde
tause stjerner besat.

Contents

List of Illustrations

Publisher's Note

The Bertolt Brecht whom Eric Bentley met in 1942 was the author of works already famous such as *Threepenny Opera* and of works to be famous later, such as *Galileo* and *Mother Courage* and *The Good Woman of Setzuan*. He had fled his native Germany in the wake of the Reichstag Fire in 1933. He spent eight years as a refugee in Scandinavia before coming to the United States in 1941. Suspected of Communist leanings, he was summoned before the House Un-American Activities Committee in 1947. Immediately thereafter he returned to Europe, first Switzerland, then East Berlin (though on an Austrian passport). He died in Berlin in 1956.

Born and brought up in England, Eric Bentley went to the USA to get a doctorate in comparative literature at Yale. While teaching at UCLA (1941-42), he met Brecht and began to translate him. Later he made the name of Brecht known in both England and America through articles, essays, lectures and above all two books: *The Playwright as Thinker* (1946) and *In Search of Theatre* (1953).

Some of Brecht's letters to Bentley, though not all, were published, in German, in the two-volume edition of Brecht letters (*Briefe*) issued in 1981. Excerpts appear in translation in Bentley's *Brecht Commentaries* (1981).

Those who seek Eric Bentley's exposition of Brecht's works, and/or his appraisal of them, should go to the last-named volume. The present volume is, as far as it could be made so, an eye-witness account of Brecht the man (over a limited period). Those who call it just a bundle of anecdotes can be referred to the words of Novalis: 'history is one great anecdote. An anecdote is an historical element, an historical molecule or epigram.'

Bentley – Bolton Wanderer

It is a little ironic that Eric Bentley should need an introduction to an English audience. The pioneer translator of Brecht who is often characterized in Britain as being too American in his use of idiom, is, in fact, an Englishman from Bolton, Lancashire. And much more than a translator and champion of Bertolt Brecht in the English-speaking world: critic, playwright, director, performer, teacher – and moulder of the taste and sensibility of several generations of readers and theatre-goers. In this wide field of unceasingly energetic activity, the encounter with Bertolt Brecht occupies an important place; and Bentley's *Brecht Memoir* can be seen as a focal point from which perspectives open up on Bentley's achievement in a number of directions.

For if Brecht had an important impact on Bentley, Bentley played an equally important part in Brecht's life in America and beyond. Bentley was far more than a mere amanuensis and helper to Brecht. He was big enough to hold his own with him and to assert his individuality and independent political point of view against the weight of that most self-righteous of geniuses.

That he could hold his own in the debate with Brecht – who either bulldozed his antagonists into the ground of total submission or reduced them to outraged and angry retreat – is an earnest of Bentley's stature. Much as he admired Brecht, he was equally incisive and illuminating as a critic and expounder of Pirandello, Strindberg, Ibsen, Shaw, Wilde, Sternheim and many other important dramatists. It was Bentley who, through his series of anthologies from the classical and modern repertoire, introduced the canon of masterworks of the European stage to America and made them available to the 'regional theatre' movement then struggling to be born in the United States. And, above all, it was Bentley who through his books and his weekly criticism diligently laboured to destroy the prevailing American presumption that the theatre is no more than a branch of the entertainment industry devoted to purvey cheap thrills, and to assert the function of drama as an instrument of serious inquiry into society and the basic problems of human existence.

In all this he has maintained a constant link between theory and practice, directing a number of the world premières of Brecht's own works; writing an impressive number of his own plays and adaptations; scoring a world-wide success with his documentary drama on the anti-Communist witch-hunt in the film industry – *Are you now or have you ever been* . . ., involving, of course, the interrogation of Bertolt Brecht; and performing his own translations of Brecht songs, accompanying himself on his rickety harmonium – perfect renderings precisely because an untrained voice and skilfully calculated 'non-professional' style provides exactly the effect Brecht himself aimed at: the spontaneity of a real person bursting into song because he wants to make a point.

Such wide-ranging achievement emphasises the fact that Eric Bentley is a prime representative of an – alas – vanishing breed of artist-critics who combine the erudition and analytical acumen of first-rate academic scholarship with the creativity that allows them to talk of art with the special insight of the practitioner, and to write their criticism in a style that bears witness to their artistry. Too much literary criticism nowadays is written so badly, in such obscurantist jargon, that it proclaims all too clearly that these critics cannot possibly be judges of good writing when they themselves so obviously have tin-ears.

Eric Bentley is one of the dwindling band of critic-scholar-artists whose work, in the tradition of the creative critics from Lessing, Coleridge, Hazlitt, to Shaw and Edmund Wilson, is readable for its own sake, able to reach the general reader, helping him towards a greater understanding and increased illumination and enjoyment of the arts. It is a saddening aspect of our times that this type of criticism now seems threatened with extinction, as the ever growing scholasticism, self-reflexiveness, and indulgence in obscurantist jargon (which merely serves to give the appearance of depth to platitudinous and shallow insights) tends to exclude all but a coterie of 'knowing' insiders.

An essential aspect of a great critic, of course, is his ability to project the image of a 'personality', so that the reader can perceive his discourse as the opinion of someone worth listening to, a voice that issues from real authority. Bentley's personality comes through, clear and strong, in everything he writes. He is a man of immense enthusiasm and commitment, forever active on behalf of causes he has embraced, or of individuals he has found worthy of support. His generosity to such individuals, his readiness to campaign on their behalf, is proverbial. The list of those who have lastingly benefited from his support and encouragement is very long. I, for one, figure on that list. I have owed him a great deal.

Bentley's *Brecht Memoir* is an expression of this aspect of his personality. It is far more than merely a contribution to the biography of a great writer. It is an immensely valuable account of the inter-action of two great personalities at a climactic period of history, at a point where two distinct cultures clashed.

MARTIN ESSLIN

Acknowledgments

The longish list of people acknowledged in *The Brecht Commentaries* might well have been reprinted here. Among these who have let me pick their brains, and invade their files, with this *Memoir* in mind, John Fuegi and James K. Lyon stand out. I enjoyed working, also, with Joel Schechter who chose to print a large portion of the *Memoir* in his magazine *Theater* at a time when I was getting the cold shoulder from other magazine editors. Elsa Lanchester graciously permitted me to print a letter to me from her late husband, Charles Laughton. David Beams provided me with yet another excellent index, not to mention his good work assisting me in other areas. Bruce Bebb pointed out that I got two addresses wrong in the Yale excerpt of the *Memoir* and gave me the appropriate corrections. Lisa Jalowetz Aronson gave me a copy of a letter from Schoenberg to her father and permission to quote it. The late Martha Feuchtwanger sent me the photo of Lion with Stalin. And, last not least, before the present Northwestern edition of this book could appear, I had to solicit and receive much expert assistance from the staff of Northwestern and of the British publisher Carcanet, not to mention my longstanding London agent, Gerald Pollinger.

E.B.
New York, November 1990

Errata

This volume has been photographically reproduced from the first British edition. The following are corrections for typographical and content errors in the original.

P. 3, line 23: "Hindenberg" should read "Hindenburg."

P. 3, line 37: "has been" should read "had been."

P. 6, line 26: "MacDonald" should read "Macdonald."

P. 11, line 32: "Thomson" should read "Thompson."

P. 26, line 25: "Lukacs" should read "Lukács."

P. 33, line 12: "Kauffmann" should read "Kaufmann."

P. 38, line 21: *"themsleves"* should read *"themselves."*

P. 45, caption: "Schoerzerkas" should read "Schweizerkas."

P. 55, line 22: "dictator-direct" should read "dictator-director."

P. 59, line 6: "Casper" should read "Caspar."

P. 79, line 6: "production" should read "reproduction."

P. 83, line 6: "acount" should read "account."

P. 103, line 23: "Kierkegaard's" should read "Montaigne's."

P. 104, line 44: "Scool" should read "School."

P. 111, line 22: *"Karamozov"* should read *"Karamazov."*

P. 114, line 2: "MacDonald" should read "Macdonald."

1

817 25th Street, Santa Monica, California, 9 June, 1942. My first meeting with Bertolt Brecht. Him, 43. Me, 25. I was teaching freshman English at UCLA and in my spare time turning my Ph.D. thesis into a book about hero worship in German and English literature. I had just discovered a German poet, Stefan George, who fleetingly became something of a hero to me: his was at the time the only photograph adorning my apartment walls in Westwood Village. My Stefan George studies led me to the home of a member of Brecht's circle of friends, the philosopher Theodor Wiesengrund Adorno, who gave me a batch of his MSS and sang me songs of his own, twelve-tone composition (the most hideous shrieks I've ever heard outside of horror movies: had he discovered a thirteenth tone?). I think I saw him only once again. That time he explained to me that *The Caucasian Chalk Circle* was not really Marxist (many people in those days explained that something or other was not really Marxist), it was, 'what do the Americans call it? Technocratic.'

One contact with new German music led to another: the Brecht composer Hanns Eisler turned up one evening in the home of a UCLA musicologist. Before he arrived, my host warned me that Eisler was the famous or was it notorious? composer of the red anthem 'Comintern' and other such scandalous items. When later we asked Hanns about these he professed to have forgotten them. 'Oh, I dashed off a number of little songs, marches and the like – that was in the fight against Hitler, before '33 – all forgotten now!' And when Stalin dissolved the Comintern in 1943, Hanns bounded to the piano and 'dissolved' his Comintern anthem in a succession of harmonies that made the original tune quite disappear.

To talk as he did, I would later learn, was a policy decision: to have a present and future in the United States, Eisler had decided to lose his past. He even seemed to believe his own fictions. I have heard him denounce the whole Brecht and Eisler *oeuvre* as mere ephemera: 'the great modern democratic

1

poet is not Brecht, it is Garcia Lorca!' But this declaration was made 'under the influence' (*in vino non veritas*), and the inebriation itself had its reasons: by then (1947) Eisler was under tremendous strain as a target of the Un-American Activities Committee and its big brazen brother the FBI. Back in 1942, he was cheerful enough and gave full play to his natural ebulliency. I recall attending a concert with him in Royce Hall, UCLA. In the intermission he spotted his old teacher Arnold Schoenberg standing in the lobby. Today, more than forty years later, I can still see those two small men with the huge eyes, Schoenberg tight – in lips and body – motionless, unsmiling, almost unspeaking – Hanns flitting about him with rapid gestures and broad smiles and a flood of flattering words.

I also retain a distinct image of Hanns at the Hollywood Hotel working at a small upright piano on a Brecht cantata. On that occasion he listened to the tale of my troubles with UCLA: I made my older colleagues jealous because I was such an eager beaver. So I was being dropped from the faculty, the reason given being that I was a scandalous character and talked about sex too much in class, too much, that was, for the taste of my Mormon and Christian Science students. Eisler proposed that I say I was suspected of Communism, and *that* was why they were laying me off. It's possible he believed this was true even though I kept telling him I wasn't even a Marxist. In Brecht circles there had to be an explanation for any problem on political lines. Hanns provided it in the present case and offered to help organize the mass movement that would 'spontaneously' rise up in my defence and result in my being re-hired . . . This idle chatter was broken up by the entry into the hotel room of another person of considerable importance in American history – and in the life of Hanns Eisler – the playwright Clifford Odets. In 1942 the relationship between those two was unshadowed. Later Odets would make 'full disclosure' of his Communist past (such as it was: it was meagre) to the Un-American Activities Committee, and Eisler would in effect declare him a non-person.

But it wasn't Adorno or Eisler who opened the 25th Street door to me, it was the movie director Herbert Kline (*Forgotten Village*), and I had come to *his* door because his wife Rosa was taking my freshman English class. I'd given her a C-minus for a paper, telling her it wasn't a critical essay as assigned, it was a *New Masses* editorial. Both the Klines then let me know that left-wing editorials met with their enthusiastic approval, and in their home I met a goodly section of Hollywood's left-wing

2

crowd, though the man who stands out in my memory was not of the Left at all. This is Max Ophuls, later the director of *La Ronde*, who talked to us one night after dinner of G. W. Pabst's (alleged) contributions to a Nazi film about the fall of France. Triumphant violence and slaughter on screen with lovely harp music on the soundtrack – I'm remembering what Ophuls said, I've no idea if it's an accurate description of the film.

It was when I was telling Herb Kline about a student of mine who had a hand printing-press and wanted to print some poems on it that the name of Brecht came up. For the first time in my life, I think. (The Brecht editor John Willett says I listened to records of *Threepenny Opera* in a college room in Oxford during the 1930s. This may well be, but I doubt that the name of its 'librettist' had made an impression.) Back in Los Angeles, Stefan George was ousted. For one thing the student-printer preferred living poets to dead ones, new poems to old. I also discovered one could not be devoted to both Stefan George and Bertolt Brecht; and my hero worship was about to be transferred from the one to the other. The photo of George would come down off my wall, and I would soon be having my own photo taken with Bertolt Brecht – by his girlfriend, Ruth Berlau.

Both George and Brecht wrote about Hindenberg. I showed Brecht my translation of George's poem, 'The War'. He laughed out loud when he came to these lines about Hindenburg: 'supported on his stick, there then descended from the colourless suburban house of the dullest of our cities a forgotten, unadorned old man: he answered the hour's need and rescued what, after all, the screamers and gesticulators had brought to the edge of the abyss: the Reich.' '*Das ist natürlich ganz albern*,' said Brecht, that, naturally, is quite fatuous.' (*Albern* and *läppisch* were favourite words of his: they both meant fatuous, silly.) It was not long since he had depicted another moment in Hindenburg's life, not 1914, but 1933, the moment when Hindenburg appointed Hitler chancellor. This was in the play *Arturo Ui*. (Another moment in Hitler's life was when, in 1944, a bomb went off that was intended to kill him. It has been placed under the table by Claus von Stauffenberg, a disciple of Stefan George.)

The house on 25th Street was small, and I was shown into Brecht's bedroom which was also his study. He had few or no books but there was a typewriter; and copies of *Freies Deutschland* – which I later found to be a Communist magazine published in Mexico City – were strewn about. In the typewriter was the very thin paper, folded double, which I later knew to be characteristic of the man. It was on this paper – the cheap tissue used for carbon copies when you have no onion skin – that I first saw any of the work of Brecht. He handed me a couple of sheets while he looked over the samples of my own work I had brought along.

My first impression of the man himself is hard to recapture at this distance in time. I believe I took Brecht for a truly proletarian writer on the score of his current lack of cash and his style of living and dress. This was naïve of me – the man was bottomlessly bourgeois – yet the charm and power of the encounter had their source in just this naïveté, and especially in the fact that I had no sense of being in the company of a famous man. Quite a contrast to those meetings with Brecht which young people were to have in the 1950s, when the cropped head and the tie-less shirt were well-known in advance from a score of photographs and a hundred anecdotes! For all I knew, Brecht might have had a trunkful of ties under the bed, and it could have been by chance that he was tie-less at the time . . . or, as I say, it could have been because he was a proletarian writer.

Most famous writers would have made sure that before I left, after our first interview, I did have a sense of their fame. Remarkable about Brecht was that he didn't bother about this. Here we see the human value of what I came later to recognize as a certain deliberate depersonalization of things which Brecht brought about. He did not try to find much out about me. He did not invite me to find out much about him. As in his plays, two people would encounter each other for the sake of what they have to do together. I was a student of German and of poetry. He was a German and had written some poems. So? *I* would translate *him*.

On the spot. And with him as collaborator. He already knew enough English to have a pretty shrewd idea if a given expression corresponded to the German. '*Wirklich, ich lebe in finsteren Zeiten!*' That was the first line on one of the bits of tissue paper he had handed me. What did it mean? 'Really, I do live in dark times'? *Finstere Zeiten* are 'dark ages'. Was the reference to *the* Dark Ages? (I had no idea of any context.) '*Nein, nein,*' said the quiet staccato voice. Then, after a puff at the cigar (not yet 'the famous cigar'), '*nein, ich meine diese Zeiten, Herr Bentley*, unsere – *auch in Los Angeles kann es finster sein, nicht wahr?*' 'No, I mean these times, Mr Bentley, ours – even in Los Angeles, it can be dark, can't it?' He was

4

teasing me. That too I would later regard as characteristic. (At least once he would refer to me as Baby-face Bentley.) At the time it was simply new . . . Well, what about *wirklich*? What did one say for that in English? 'Actually', 'of course', 'oh, yes', 'it's true'? To each of these suggestions of mine, the quiet, sharp voice said '*Nein! Nein!*' And Brecht shook his head decisively. We were discovering together that, in our effort to translate his poetry, we could not get past the very first word.

Maybe I didn't yet know enough German? I was still taking courses in that language (at UCLA). When Brecht first heard me speak his native language, he smiled. I blushed: 'Do I sound that bad?' 'On the contrary,' said he, 'you sound that beautiful! You speak the language of Goethe and Heine, only slightly corrupted by Stefan George, and of course even *his* language is "beautiful" too!' All my German at that time came out of books – good books, luckily. 'We don't speak beautiful German any more,' says Brecht, 'we all sound like the Führer!'

At subsequent sessions, he read his poems back at me. He may have read slowly because he doubted my ability to follow if he read fast, but in any event what I remember is the loving care which his quiet, thin voice lavished upon each word. Compared with George, the poetry, too, seemed quiet and thin. Incidentally, I was taken aback at the word Housepainter in this poetry – as a standard way of referring to Hitler. Was this just *Daily Worker* cartoons in verse? Was it poetry destined to live and quietly die in *The New Masses*?

Der Anstreicher spricht von kommenden grossen Zeiten
Die Wälder wachsen noch
Die Äcker tragen noch
Die Städte stehen noch
Die Menschen atmen noch.

The housepainter speaks of the great times to come
The forests are still growing
The fields are still bearing fruit
The cities are still standing
The people are still breathing.

Brecht made a long pause at the end of every line, letting the images hang in the air. What he wanted me to realize, he said, before I started translating, was that this writing was '*ungeheuer delikat*'. 'Frightfully delicate' the phrase surprised me at the time for the left-wing talk I had heard was all for

5

blunt forthrightness, even when it was not positively hostile to beauty and refinement.

Poetry, says Robert Frost, is what does not come through in translation. This truth was empirically established by Brecht and myself, but luckily it is a truth which all are agreed in advance to defy, and a half-truth at that. A lot of poetry just as problematical as Brecht's has come down to us in more languages than one – with whatever changes along the way . . . Although something must have happened to my student's hand-press, for I never saw anything in print from it, I had begun the 'impossible' task: translating poetry, translating Bertolt Brecht.

For a while nothing was said about publication, but then Brecht wanted his poem 'To the German Soldiers in the East' to be printed. With him it was always a matter of the place and the time to publish something, considered not personally or 'literarily', but politically. People in America should now read what he had to say about the German soldiers in World War II (which, perhaps consciously, was the opposite of what George had said of the German soldiers in World War I.) So I translated that poem and sent it to *Partisan Review*. The choice was politically inept since the *PR* people were violently anti-Communist, but then, being anti-Communist (i.e. formerly Communist), they knew about Brecht. In fact they had run a 'big' article about him by Clement Greenberg (not yet a famous art critic) in 1941. So I was upset when Dwight MacDonald (not yet a famous movie critic), rejecting the poem for the magazine, told me how outrageous he considered its sentiments to be. (The Germans were barbarians at the gates of a super-civilized Russia . . . In 1965 an editor of *Partisan* was to ask me please not to fight the Cold War when criticizing the Brecht theatre in East Berlin. Maybe it's good that times change?) 'To the German Soldiers in the East' appeared in *The Rocky Mountain Review*, late 1943.

For me T. W. Adorno had been the link between Stefan George and Bertolt Brecht. He was also a link between Arnold Schoenberg and Bertolt Brecht. From 1942 I taught at the much discussed progressive school, Black Mountain College in North Carolina. At that school, my guide, philosopher and friend was a Schoenberg protégé, Heinrich Jalowetz.[1] It was Jalowetz who gave me an introduction to the Viennese poet and stage director, Berthold Viertel – the 'Bergmann' of Christopher Isherwood's novel *Prater Violet*. In June 1942 Viertel directed scenes from Brecht's *The Private Life of the*

Master Race in German at the Barbizon Plaza Hotel in New York: Herbert Berghof was in it. Later that year Viertel gave me a copy of the German script they had used and told me Brecht wanted me to translate it. It was my second real commission. The first was to translate *Tales from the Vienna Woods* by Odön von Horváth for a refugee producer, or would-be producer, named Leo Mittler. Nothing came of this, and my translation is lost. I got no money either from Mittler or Brecht but I was thrilled by both commissions and had soon finished work on *Master Race*. A staged reading was presented at the College, 26 February, 1944. Fritz Cohen, formerly of the Ballet Jooss, later of Juilliard, was at the Hammond organ with a splendidly distorted harmonization of the Horst Wessel Lied. That April, Radio Station WWNC in Asheville broadcast our performance, and around this time Jay Laughlin of New Directions accepted the play for book publication.

On 22 December 1943, the tenth anniversary of the Reichstag Fire Trial was commemorated in Carnegie Hall. The whole political spectrum from the Fascist Batista to the Communist Browder was represented. Brecht read a statement in my translation. Later I wondered about a comment on this text to the effect that it was in excellent English. BB's advice to me had been: 'Don't make the English too good. It should have a German accent, *nicht wahr? Ich bin kein 100% Amerikaner, wie?* – I'm not a hundred per cent American, understand?'

The statement was one of two pieces Brecht had me translate around that time in defence of the current Communist line on Germany. (The German people were anti-Nazi. Army divisions much needed on the Russian front had to be left at home to keep the people in line . . .) Brecht said that with the help of the novelist Lion Feuchtwanger, his friend and collaborator, I could get the second and longer piece published in *The Saturday Evening Post*. Actually, I could get no magazine to publish it at the time. A little later the Party changed its mind about the German people – they weren't undiscourageable democrats, their minds had been poisoned by Fascism – and the piece ceased to be what was called in Brecht circles *aktuell* – topical. Indeed, Brecht lost the original German MS, and the item survived only in my English translation.

That the Communist Party could go so fast from one view of German character to its opposite has been taken as mere opportunism. But a radical uncertainty existed all along, and would continue to exist in the future. I noticed it in Brecht. On the one hand, he would preach, 'Trust the people', and prate confidently of the *Weisheit des Volkes*. On the other hand, on the least provocation, he would angrily give up the German people as hopeless, 'and I know my Germans', etcetera.

There was an 'on the other hand' also to his anti-Americanism. If the Americans, too, were hopeless, they were also not so hopeless, and were to be distinguished from their more completely hopeless Ruling Class. They were human, and he liked some of their habits so much he affected them: not shaking hands upon being introduced, for example, or saying 'so what?', an expression that did not exist in German until Brecht first said, 'so was?'

Lion Feuchtwanger, Stalin, and B. M. Tal, editor of Pravda. *In Brecht's circle, only Feuchtwanger seems to have got into the actual presence of Stalin. This was because he had been chosen to make the official retort to André Gide on the subject of freedom in the U.S.S.R. Viking Press published the result in the book* Moscow 1937.

Eric Bentley, c. 1940　　　　*Elisabeth Hauptmann, c. 1930*

817 25th Street, Santa Monica, where Bentley first met Brecht

Berthold Viertel drawn by B. F. Dolbin

2

*Lexington Avenue and 23rd Street, New York, 12 June 1945,
the world première of Brecht's* Master Race *in an auditorium
belonging to City College.* The words 'New York' bring up
other topics and particularly Brecht's old friend (= former
girlfriend) Elisabeth Hauptmann, who was living at 243
Riverside Drive. 'She can't say "it's raining" without looking
over her shoulder to see if J. Edgar Hoover is eavesdropping.'
This is what I was told of Frau Hauptmann by another German
woman, Therese Pol, daughter of the composer Paul Dessau,
a report which is not really to Frau Hauptmann's discredit
since, in the light of the Freedom of Information Act, we know
now that J. Edgar Hoover generally *was* eavesdropping. But
paranoia is still paranoia even when provoked.

At the time I used to visit her regularly on Riverside Drive,
Frau Hauptmann was masterminding a magazine pleasantly
entitled *The Protestant*. She told me how glad she would be
to arrange for me to write for it: it was the most progressive
magazine in America. Looking through a few back issues,
I noticed that it was not the most Protestant magazine in
America.

Frau Hauptmann was also masterminding Dorothy Thompson,
then possibly the most influential columnist in the country. The
needed intermediary between these two powerful females was a
male Communist named Hermann Budzislavsky – later a VIP in
East Germany – who had contrived to become Ms Thompson's
'private secretary'. When I turned up at the Hauptmann apartment for a Brecht session, Frau Hauptmann would be on the
phone telling *lieber Budzi* what should be in the next Thompson
column, and a few days later I would see that it *was* said in that
column.

If Dorothy Thompson's politics were 'corrected' by Frau
Hauptmann, Ms Thomson didn't know it and was furious
when, later, she found out. But Bertolt Brecht's lines were
sometimes corrected by Frau Hauptmann, and it was fine
with him. 'Yes, yes,' he would tell me, 'let that stand.' In

my opinion, she ruined one scene in *The Private Life of the Master Race* and her handiwork still stands in the editions, German and English. It was a scene presenting the terrible fact that the Communists fought with the Social Democrats even in the Nazi camps. The original scene presented simply the horror and irony. Frau Hauptmann didn't buy that. With her, policy and ideology came before facts and loyalty to them. We were having a United Front at the time – well, weren't we? Of course. 'We' Communists were working with 'us' Social Democrats. Of course we were. Therefore what must happen is that the quarrellers become friends when threatened by the Nazis. Friends and heroes to boot, since they were to refuse, on pain of torture, to give each other away. Only a few lines needed to be added to the scene, so it was a heroism achieved with a minimum of labour. Brecht brought the lines in the following day, and I translated them:

> (*SS Guard appears.*)
> GUARD: You people have learned nothing. Who was it shouted 'You betrayed the people'?
> (*No one speaks.*)
> GUARD: We'll shove you in the bunker till you pass out. I'll give you five seconds to speak up. Then the bunker!
> (*Five seconds of silence.*)

It had been the Communists who said, 'You betrayed the people'. The Social Democrats decline to turn him in.

Frau Hauptmann also took it as her function to adapt the play to local conditions and assumptions. A Brechtian hero faces death and leaves a message for the son who will survive him: 'Be true to your class.' But in 1944 people like *lieber Budzi* were taking over Vice-President Henry Wallace who had announced that ours will prove to be the century, not of the proletariat, but of the common man. So I was instructed by Frau Hauptmann that my American text would read: 'Be true to the common people.' And the line remains to haunt me because some years later when I went down to the East Village to see a performance of the play, a shrill voice in the theatre lobby reached my ears: 'Bentley obviously doesn't know German, he has translated the word that means "class" as "common people"!' It was a German-speaking person denouncing me to the management. (He may also have been an FBI man. Walter Winchell had announced on the radio

12

that Bertolt Brecht would be present and make a speech that night. The FBI sent someone to check it out. He reported that the speaker was not Brecht but Professor Eric Bentley of Columbia University. There were only about a dozen people in the house.)

Frau Hauptmann also made a suggestion that throws a certain light upon Brechtian theatre as a whole. The scenes of life in Germany under the Nazis were all written, but she proposed that I go to the 42nd Street Library and find documents on which they might *seem* to have been based. Had I done so, the play would have become one hundred per cent authentic, historical, truly a Living Newspaper. Each scene was to be headed by a relevant eye-witness account or legal document but, whether from laziness or disinclination, I never got around to what would have been quite a problematic piece of research; and the scenes have yet to receive such 'authentication'.

Early in 1945, when I was teaching in Minneapolis, and Brecht was living in California, we received an offer from an off-Broadway production outfit entitled The Theatre of All Nations. Brecht was later to comment, with reason, that this number of nations was too many for the purpose, but *The Private Life of the Master Race* was produced and the prospects originally seemed good. Erwin Piscator, the eminent German director whose name people associated with Brecht's, though actually he had never directed any of Brecht's plays, was to direct, and the great Albert Bassermann would appear in the cast. However, by the time I got in from Minnesota, Piscator had quarrelled with Brecht and had been replaced by Berthold Viertel. When I entered the Brecht-Berlau apartment, 124 East 57th Street, Brecht was on the phone, yelling about one of his favourite subjects: 'Verbrecher' – crooks. Evidently the voice at the other end had spoken of the producers as Big Crooks because Brecht was yelling: 'No, no, no, *little* crooks – we can't even sue them to any good effect!'

Brecht would always shout and scream when things went wrong in the theatre. His paranoia was as outrageous as that of anyone I've ever met with the single exception, perhaps, of the critic F. R. Leavis. He found hostility and sabotage every-where, and, though often he didn't know who the 'enemies' were, he wouldn't hesitate to define them as Nazis. Sometimes he would claim that the rows he made were part of a deliberate plan to improve standards. This claim only made his wild accusations the more unconscionable, yet there was something suspicious in the speed with which the screaming maniac could become a good imitation of a wimp. ('Thou whose exterior semblance doth belie/Thy soul's immensity!') That is how he looked, at least to the casual observer, in the Lexington Avenue bus after rehearsal in the grey workshirt worn, student fashion, outside the pants and the peaked cap that was supposed to make him look like a Worker but actually made him look a shade mousy, not to mention the three-days' growth of hair often on his chin. Probably the younger generation in the 1980s finds this last feature rather dashing, but in the 1940s the unshaven look was not chic.

Remarkable how Brecht could blend with the world of lower-class Manhattan – the subways, the buses – and yet be at heart so thoroughly alien from it. I retain an image of him sitting silently in a half-empty IRT subway train, rather late at night, idly scanning the headline of a paper being read by someone opposite. Referring to the Polish 'government in exile' in London, it ran: POLES REJECT RED BORDER. Brecht nodded, a tired smile on his lips, and said in his very distinct English with its Germanic guttural R's: 'Rrred borrrder rrreject Poles!'

The Private Life of the Master Race was so bad that Brecht wanted to prevent it from opening. As the Author, and this no doubt was very European of him, he expected to be the autocrat of the breakfast table. Contracts could be torn up, he assumed, at will. New York had news for him: once he had signed a contract he had ceded many of his powers. This powerlessness, the feeling of it, greatly exacerbated his natural paranoia. 'If I can't stop the show, I'll exclude all critics! Viertel, arrange with Bentley to keep all critics out!' His idea was now that if his producer would not act on his behalf, those closer to him would. But we couldn't. And then that sabotage which Brecht was so willing to accuse others of was practised by the Meister himself. The actress playing his Jewish Wife couldn't be replaced? Then he'd fix *her*. 'Give Viertel these revisions!' The 'revisions' were simply cuts. Any parts of the dialogue he thought were handled badly he cut right out: they amounted to at least half the scene. Dramaturgy was no longer a consideration. The scene was now such that the audience wouldn't be able to follow it. Important was only to destroy the actress and defy the producer.

The opening night was a fiasco. Brechtian devices such as would be declared brilliant a few years later all over Western Europe came off awkward and sophomoric: for example, an SS Man played by a black actor in white face.

An ill-prepared orchestra in the pit stumbled through Eisler's parodies of Nazi band music: it sounded as if they were trying to play the real thing but failing. Elisabeth Bergner sat in the wings and wept. Viertel and myself, in the back row with many empty rows in front of us, applauded at every opportunity with simulated enthusiasm.

Jay Laughlin took some of us out for a beer afterwards and announced that all the copies of the book of the play which he had sent for sale in the lobby had been stolen – by the producer? Next morning, except for the mild Lewis Nichols in *The New York Times*, the reviewers chirped and chortled at that which always brings sunshine into their bleak souls: the failure of something 'highbrow'. Brecht asked Ruth Berlau to have all the reviews cut out for publication in his collected works later.

Like all theatre people, Brecht could assume for the moment that nothing in the whole world mattered except what was happening on a stage in his own show, yet he differed from most playwrights in not assuming that the failure of a production was the failure of a play. Also, his political activities, while they paused, did not totally stop because there was a show on. One day, when I turned up at 124 East 57th Street, a compact, rather other-wordly gentleman was just leaving. 'That was Dr Paul Tillich,' Brecht said. I asked what *he* – a Protestant theologian – could be doing here. Brecht sternly gave me to understand that he and Tillich were busy building a New Germany. Yes, Tillich was a social democrat but 'I,' said Brecht, 'always tried to be the link between Communism and Social Democracy.' (Actually, he tried never to say anything bad about Communism or anything good about Social Democracy: that was how United Fronts, in those days, got to be United.) Years later Mrs Tillich was to tell me Brecht had worked hard on converting Paul *from* Social Democracy *to* Communism (There are churchmen in East Germany today who support the Communist regime. What a coup for Brecht if he could have won a 'star' like Tillich to support the CP cause!)

German Communists in New York did not always support the cause of Bertolt Brecht. I had got to know Franz Weiskopf – a Czech national who wrote in German and attended meetings of what I took to be German CP functionaries – at a time when he wanted me to translate him – a project that didn't work out since for some reason I was not acceptable to his publishers,

Alfred A. Knopf Inc. But I used to get invited to his apartment where I drank in the atmosphere. It was there that I learned, though I hardly knew it at the time, the true relation between orthodox Communist writers and Brecht. The fact was that *some* of Brecht's work was considered very fine. 'But a lot of it,' Weiskopf said quite flatly, 'is shit.' He went on to assure me, since I was Brecht's translator, that, in the interests of solidarity, he would never reveal this publicly.

On the contrary, he gave a party for Brecht, I remember, a nice, down-at-heel party, in his nice, down-at-heel Greenwich Village apartment, with the one picture on the wall, a cartoon by Arthur Szyk of Hitler getting his comeuppance, stuck into the plaster with thumb tacks. (Another Szyk cartoon inspired a large part of Brecht's *Schweyk*.) An inner circle of young left-wingers knew who and what Brecht was and sat at his feet. He took such things in stride, and mildly told us that Schoenberg had made a contribution to music in his day but that, of course, Eisler had now gone far beyond him. Considering that most of us hadn't heard of Eisler that was quite a testimonial. I never knew, and still don't, whether Brecht believed what he was saying. I soon learned, however, that in his swaggering vein he was given to pronouncements of this sort.

He would swagger more freely in Ruth's apartment than away from home, and he would swagger more freely with an audience of one – such as myself, with Ruth bobbing in and out – than in company. By 'swagger' I mean: pace to and fro waving that cigar and getting himself excited. Under such circumstances the topic would turn to himself – where else? If I had ventured on the word Creative, he would toss off: 'Anyone can be creative, it's re-writing other people that's a challenge.' (At a later time, he came up with a corollary. Because the lyrics to *Galileo* had first been written in English, he had the job of translating them into German – to fit music composed to fit the English. He was sweating as he listened to the music and toyed with the syllables and accents. Translator now, not creator, he turned to me and said: 'I now know your job is harder than mine.') He would complain that Thomas Mann has (allegedly: I never heard it confirmed from any other source) described him as '*der leider sehr begabte Brecht*', 'the unfortunately very gifted Brecht.' 'And their rules and criteria,' he was addressing himself now to teachers and critics, knowing that I myself was both, 'they can all be ignored, defied, and should be. Climax two thirds of the way through? Unity of action? Who says so? *They* say so. I say: Why?' On the other side, when he heard someone had said his *Galileo didn't* have unity of action, was amorphous and 'episodic', he was eager to exclaim: 'Just the contrary! They think I just meander along, stick things in at random. Actually, I work from a chart posted on the wall. I connect everything with everything else. D'you see the connection between the first scene and the last? In both, Galileo is *imbibing*, milk in the beginning, a goose at the end. Because he is the same man: greedy . . . Of course you only appreciate this the *second* time you see the first scene. The second time is the first time you really "see" a play! So don't ask what I think of your critics who never see a play more than once! Today's critics! Today's society! Only when there's a socialist world will there be a world for *my* work!'

It was sometime in 1945 that my first book on the drama was accepted for publication by a newish firm in New York, Reynal and Hitchcock Inc. I suggested that they publish the collected works of Brecht, and they picked up the suggestion. I was to be general editor, though, on the insistence of Brecht, I had to accept the collaboration of the formidable Frau Hauptmann.

My book *The Playwright as Thinker* infuriated Erwin Piscator who wrote me, in a letter dated 27 May 1946:

> . . . the one-sidedness of your description [of me] may be very dangerous for me at the present time. If you were older, riper, and more realistic I could perhaps ask you, 'How much money did you receive for sending out such a "steckbrief" for a refugee or such a political defamation?'

But Brecht was interested enough to accept my proposal that we embark upon a publishable correspondence about theatre with my book as point of departure. I wished to challenge the excessive claims for the theory of Epic Theatre which Brecht had made earlier in his career; and eventually he did claim less and did present a far less heretical view of dramatic art. However, he was not ready to do this in 1946, and the correspondence broke off. The answer came two years later in the form of a long essay entitled a 'Short Organum', which I forthwith arranged to have translated by one of my graduate students and brought out in *Accent* magazine.

It was in the mid 1940s that Brecht gained some slight acquaintance with Broadway. On the whole, he was not amused. Even by *The Glass Menagerie*, one of the best American plays of that time. Or by what may have been *the* best: *The Iceman Cometh*. 'If you open a play with the image of a roomful of sleeping men,' said BB, 'the audience will take the hint.' He *was* amused by Orson Welles in the Cole Porter musical, *Around the World*, but, failing to discern any colour scheme in the costumes and sets, declared Americans colour blind. Ingrid Bergman? Even those who did not applaud her acting in *Joan of Lorraine* praised her beauty. Brecht found her 'ugly as night'. He enjoyed rejecting Nordic models, and gloried in what was blatantly non-Aryan. Parallel to the racial bias was the social. Aristocracies are bad; peasantries are good, if poor enough. Therefore the former are ugly, the latter, beautiful. In clothing as well as in face. In Brecht plays, the good guys wear the browns and greys of the peasantry; the bad guys, the bright and brilliant colours of the aristocracy. If you took up such themes with Brecht in conversation, as many of us did, he would point out that we have let Italian Renaissance painters dictate our criteria of feminine beauty. He commended to us – the women of Africa.

Brecht regarded the Federal Theatre (1936-9) as the best news there had ever been about theatre in America. 'In America,' he said, 'things are better when they're worse. What the American theatre needs today [1947] is another Depression. When Americans are prosperous, theatre is something they can't afford.' He would sometimes claim that he liked American musical comedy. He had seen very little of it. And what he conceived it to be like one can deduce from the fact that he regarded his own *Caucasian Chalk Circle* as a contribution to the American musical stage.

3

Meanwhile Back in Berlin. Behind him in Germany Brecht, in 1933, had left his elder son, his elder daughter, his father, his brother, various ex-girlfriends, and some of his closest friends and co-workers, such as the stage designer Caspar Neher and the stage director Erich Engel. So he was hardly in a position to argue, as many refugees did, that people had either to leave Germany or resign themselves to being regarded as Nazis. Some of his closest associates, notably the playwright Arnolt Bronnen and the actor Heinrich George, did support the Nazis. I never heard him speak of them, though I know he denounced George in a poem – one of those exercises in grandiose self-righteousness which Communist culture delights in. Supporters of Stalin have still not been treated that roughly. Also, Brecht didn't treat all Nazi-supporters alike. The critic Herbert Ihering was excused, yet he had praised the regime in fulsome terms in a book he wrote on the actor Emil Jannings (and, for all I know, elsewhere). What excused him was that he had been such a good friend to Brecht, being the first critic to recognize his genius. I mention this less to fault Brecht than to show that, in a pinch, his criteria were not political. The *terms* in which I heard him excuse Ihering were as follows: 'Well, *wissen Sie*, Ihering was never a Marxist. He wasn't Jewish. He was a *Berliner*. A fixture in Berlin – like a lamp-bracket on a Berlin apartment wall.' I asked BB if he had read Ihering's book on Jannings – I had managed to root out a copy in a bookshop, though someone solicitous for Ihering had torn out the title page where his name must have appeared. 'No: but I'm sure that what he said in favour of the Nazis was the absolute minimum. Just enough to preserve his . . . place on the wall.'

Brecht as Stalin, Santa Monica [1943?]

Caspar Neher

Peter Lorre, c. 1935

The Laughton connection [1947?]

Hanns Eisler at Malibu, 1946
(photo: Gerda Goedhart, courtesy of Hanns Eisler Archives)

4

The Coronet Theatre, Los Angeles, California, 31 July 1947. Let me drop some names: I was seated beside Peter Lorre, behind Ingrid Bergman, and in front of Charlie Chaplin. Lorre alone would have been enough: he is probably the most intelligent actor I have ever met, even making allowances for the fact that, in front of the young Professor Bentley, he too much enjoyed showing off his erudition. (*'Was sagt Heidegger dazu?'* – 'What does Heidegger say to that?') It is the first night of *Galileo*, and Lorre is telling me how *he* would do the play, how he would do other Brecht plays, and, yes, he would do *all* of them, he has known since the 1920s that BB is *the* dramatist, *the* poet, of our day . . . Brecht is nervous just before curtain time. He runs out of the theatre to the nearest drugstore, exclaiming: *'Ich muss ein Seven Up haben'* – I must have a Seven Up.'

I had been staying at Jay Laughlin's ski lodge in Utah, and drove down to L.A. with Maja, my wife and collaborator. The Brechts put us up in their garden house. I recall that the walls of the bathroom had been papered by Brecht's wife Helene Weigel with Chinese newspapers. She was an excellent cook and a hospitable hostess. Bourgeois regularity? No. Brecht led a double life which made him hard to keep tabs on. He might be at his family place for supper, but he had installed Ruth Berlau in a house a mile or two off, and he would characteristically repair to her place during the evening, very likely returning 'home' in the morning to work in his study. Maja and I would be driven between one house and the other at need, occasionally taking in a call at the Peter Lorre residence which was on a grand scale. Horses! For Lorre, to be a star was to have one's own stable. He also had his own Frau Hauptmann on the premises. No, not as mistress, but as counsellor and friend: she called the position 'private secretary'. (What is a public secretary?)

Slightly unnerving, chez Brecht, the comings and goings. Only Helene Weigel seemed to have settled in, to really reside there. How she managed to cook for people who showed up at different and unpredictable times one never knew. The son and daughter – Stefan and Barbara – were already showing the symptoms of whatever that malady should be called from which the children of the conspicuous so often suffer. Signs of strain, of wear and tear, and, yes, of rebelliousness . . .

It seemed hard for Brecht to sit through a meal with family and guests. He would flee to his room before dessert. One would discover at some point that he had run to his couch and a detective novel. (He read them in English, his command of the language being much greater than people thought who heard him speak it.)

The rebelliousness of the Brecht children has its importance for the student of Brecht: the children were the only channel through which rebellion could come to Brecht and stay. He would meet with someone like Ruth Fischer, née Eisler, rebel against Stalinism, call her a swine and prescribe that she be shot. One of this son's friends was a son of Viertel named Hans who reports that Brecht would shout that *he* should be shot, repeating the key word several times: shot, shot, shot! Hans adds, however, that this was only when carried away and that Brecht didn't really mean it: he was very friendly to Hans later. That is the point. He would let the children rebel. He would say he wouldn't, but still he did. About such as Fischer, there can be little doubt that, if empowered, he *would* have condemned her to death. Treason to the Soviet Union was treason *tout court*; only slowly, and at that incompletely, did BB come to see Stalin himself as traitor, 'honoured murderer of the people'. Stefan Brecht and Hans Viertel were 'Trotskyites' (perhaps the 'quotes' are uncalled for) who had to be tolerated even in a home where tolerance was not preached. They helped to prevent Bertolt Brecht's mind from becoming entirely closed.

Strange how little has been said by memoirists and biographers about Brecht as a father.[2] Even I, who was not in the Brecht home often, have some vivid memories. Item: His daughter Barbara (this was in Zurich, and she was a young woman now) slamming the door of her room on both parents as she shrieked: 'You can take your social significance and shove it!' Item: BB asking me to send money (this in Munich later still) to his son Stefan and adding rather savagely: 'Why do I send it? He'll probably spend it on whores.'

A 'bad father', then, like many another writer? Yet a 'correct', bourgeois father in the end, for, in his will, he did not order his estate on the *Chalk Circle* principle of 'to those who can best use it', but left everything to his widow, the other women in his life (past and present), and the three surviving children. (The full story of the will – or rather, wills – is too long to tell here and even now, 1988, not all the facts are known.)

Helene Weigel held open house every Sunday evening. They were very nice occasions socially, unpretentious, warm, with beer and an item or two of Weigel's cooking. Hostess was a very good role for this actress, even if Host was not something her husband could bring himself to be. He would deposit himself in a corner where people had to come and seek him out, whereas she would flit about and make sure that any who felt unwelcome changed their minds. The guests were mainly German, and most of the conversation was in that language, but two types of people were present and no more: those for whom Communism was the answer to everything, and unpolitical people from theatre and film like Charles Laughton. Peter Lorre was a necessary guest as being maybe the only one who comfortably straddled the two worlds, as well as being fluent both in German and English. In memory stays a moment when the words 'Der Kommunismus' rang out loud and clear and was followed by a knock on the door. Conversation stopped. Had the FBI heard the word and sprung into action? In strides a round little man with a broad ironic smile and very keen eyes. 'Der Kommunismus?' he asks loudly, 'der Kommunismus?' It is Peter Lorre.

Brecht left America the year before Henry Wallace ran for president but the Wallace movement was under way and Brecht saw the imminent campaign as the Final Conflict. 'It's Wallace or World War III!' he would exclaim and look you challengingly in the eye. The apocalyptic character of the man's vision relieved him of all liberal illusions about the Nazis: he was convinced from the outset that they would draw the line nowhere. In some of his moods he would describe all friends of capitalism as Nazis. When I told him I was flying to Europe by Youth Argosy, an outfit that arranged cheap chartered flights for students and was having difficulty getting recognition in the airports, Brecht was immediately certain that the major airlines would arrange for a Youth Argosy plane to sink in Mid-Atlantic. He gravely advised that I make other arrangements.

And my own relation to this milieu? In Brecht's eyes at the time, I *had* to be seen as belonging, like his friend Laughton, to the unpolitical men, the uninstructed, the naïve. There was no alternative except to be 'one of us'. Because I saw no purpose in a pretense of argument (real argument being excluded, certainly), I allowed myself to be placed in this category, as far as BB himself was concerned. But I tried to get a point through to him that I might be of importance. My sense was that, if his allegiance to the Soviet Union was strong, his allegiance to his own literary career and destiny was even stronger. Though I knew I would not persuade him to admit as much, I felt that I might get through to him if I said: 'Whatever the validity of Marxism or Stalinism, if we wish to make a future for your work in America, it must be through your cogency as an artist, not your rightness as a philosopher.' I was able to tell Brecht that most of the ideas in his 'Short Organum' were not dependent on Marxism, let alone Stalinism, for their validation.

Not that, even in those early years, I ever fully saw myself as a champion of the 'Organum' or of any of Brecht's theoretical writings. Even he never realized this but thanked me as late as 1949 for being, apparently, not only a champion but *the* champion of his 'theory'. His antipathy for individualism was such, I suppose, that he could not conceive that anyone might wish to champion, not a theory, or its philosophical background, but a practice, a person practising. Am I saying that I was impressed not by Marx and Stalin but by Brecht? Not that, either. Marxism was important to me. I was and am deeply influenced by it. But I have never been a Marxist. On Stalin, like some others, I had no consistent position, but this was a period when Winston Churchill himself could speak quite loudly of 'Stalin the Great' and, at a time when I abandoned pacifism for support of the Allied cause in World War II, I too did some blathering of this sort. The curious can find a little such blather in my first book, which came out in 1944, and which caused me to be labelled a Stalinist by Philip Rahv, Sidney Hook and many others. I mention this here, however, only in order to make, yes, 'full disclosure', and not because my short-lived approval of Stalin had much bearing on my continuing relation with Brecht. He never noticed my limited and ephemeral support for Russia. What he noticed was that I was never a Marxist; what he thought he noticed was that I championed his ideas about theatre; and what he perhaps failed to notice was that I was championing his work, his genius, and therefore himself. The Communists in New York, like Weiskopf, were telling me: 'Brecht is good insofar he is Communist', but what I was privately concluding was that Brecht was good insofar as he was Brecht. (And he was not Brecht completely. Sometimes he was just Marxism or some other *ism*. And then, according to me, he was less good.)

Though young and in many ways diffident, I even tried to influence Brecht. I hoped to broaden his mind, though I knew he held what the rest of us regard as breadth of mind in contempt. 'Broadminded people,' he said once, 'see three points for and three points against every proposition. The two sides cancel out. Three minus three is zero . . . ' What I had read of the left-wing controversy over Realism rather bored me, and I realize now it should have bored me – or bothered me – utterly. Each of those wretched writers sought to take Realism and ram it down your throat. And while the 'discussion' was null and void intellectually, it was dynamite politically: say the wrong thing and you went (if you lived in Russia anyway) straight to the Gulag or to the next world . . . Of course I did not know the political dimensions of the situation in the early 1940s but, recognizing intellectual emptiness when I saw it, I (1) resolved to omit the word Realism entirely from my book-length account of modern drama (*The Playwright as Thinker*),[3] and (2) sent Brecht a copy of *Mimesis* by Erich Auerbach, a book which makes a supremely rational use of the word Realism. I'd be surprised to hear that he ever read one word of it. The critical works at hand, when I visited Brecht later, were by his old adversary, and long time slave of Stalin, Georg Lukacs, who probably did more than any other critic to empty the word Realism of meaning.

Charles Laughton. He, of course, was the star of *Galileo* and the latest man of power who was supposed to give BB the status he felt he was entitled to. A very strong mutual admiration society was created. No praise for Mr Laughton could be too high in the opinion of Mr Brecht. No praise for Mr Brecht could be too high in the opinion of Mr Laughton. 'I believe him to be the most important living dramatist,' Laughton wrote me, adding in a postscript: 'This is pretty strong and you could never print this but I believe there is Shakespeare and then Brecht.'

That was in 1948. As yet Laughton could not believe Brecht and Eisler were really identified with the Communist movement. When FBI men haunted the Maxine Elliot Theatre in '47, he couldn't 'for the life of him' tell why. 'Eisler, a Communist? Nonsense: his music is just like Mozart!' But the times they were a-changin', and even such as Charles Laughton saw, if not the light, then the darkness. He *had* associated with Communists, but please teacher, he didn't mean to! What could he do to atone? Repent? What was Galileo's word: recant? He would do it. He would espouse the New Conservatism. He would direct a play with a different message indeed from what those rebels preached: *The Caine Mutiny Court Martial*. Even when the captain is a dangerous nut, a crew has no right to rebel because it's more important that authority should be respected than that justice should be done. Questioned about this by the press, Laughton simply declared, 'them's my sentiments'. So when *Time* magazine ran a cover story on Laughton (31 March 1952), and portraits were included of all the great men he had portrayed, there was an omission: Galileo Galilei. And if Laughton repudiated Brecht, Brecht repudiated Laughton in an epigram: 'Speak now of the weather and bury that man for me deep in the earth who, before he'd spoken, took it back.'

Actually, Laughton took nothing back: he hadn't been on the point of speaking. This friendship was all public relations, though not without its humanity. Laughton could get so tired of luxury that he'd foresake his gourmet cook and run over to the Brechts' where 'Helli' would fix him a chop. But he was never accepted, chez Brecht, as what he was: a man trying to be honestly homosexual. (Honestly? Well, as much as was possible in those days without risking instant ruin. On a movie set, in front of the crew and a large crowd of extras, a director had shouted, 'Charles, Charles, *must* you come on as a flaming queen?' and Charles had answered by extending his middle finger and shouting back, 'Sometimes, my dear man, even in Hollywood, the truth will out!')

Charles had got his boyfriend cast as Andrea – the second-best part in Galileo. The boyfriend didn't deserve the part as I pointed out to Ruth Berlau. She agreed. She told me everyone agreed, including the nominal director, Joseph Losey. 'Then why isn't he replaced?' 'Because,' Ruth told me, 'Brecht doesn't want to hear about such things.' 'But you – you could talk to him!' 'No, no!' 'Surely he wants the best actor for the part?' 'No. This is a subject that cannot be brought up in Brecht's presence.' Curious: because, otherwise, Brecht was a single-minded champion of his own interests. (Soviet Communism is homophobic, and even T. W. Adorno said 'totalitarianism and homosexuality belong together.')

The full text of Charles Laughton's letter quoted above reads as follows:

My dear Bentley:

I owe you many apologies for not replying to your appeals about Brecht before.

I believe him to be the most important living dramatist. At the same time, I have never been able to understand either yours or anybody else's translations of his plays. As far as I have got is to be able to dimly see the great architecture. I also understand that you didn't like my translation of *Galileo*, so the situation between us is not an easy one. If I allow you to say, 'I believe Berthold Brecht to be the most important living dramatist', and if the general public is anything like myself, they will see my name stuck on something they cannot understand, which is somewhat of a black eye for me. At the same time I feel all kinds of a heel that I am not doing everything I possibly can for this great writer. I would certainly like to be a help, and not a hindrance.

Suggestions, please, and very warmest personal regards.

Sincerely yours,
Charles Laughton

P.S. I also feel that the actors as a whole failed this great man miserably in our production of *Galileo*. The demands he makes on actors are much the same as the demands that Shakespeare made on the actors in the Elizabethan days. This is pretty strong and you could never print this, but I believe there is Shakespeare, and then Brecht. To this end I have started a Shakespearian group, training a bunch of American actors and actresses in the business of verse speaking and prose speaking. We have been working together some 8 or 9 months, three evenings a week for three hours, and I believe that in another year (it will take no more, but will also take no less) we shall be the best team of speakers in the English language. I am doing this solely with the aim of getting a company together that can play Brecht's plays. I want to see *Galileo really* performed, and *Circle of Chalk* and *Mother Courage*, and the rest of them. I am devoting all my spare energies to that end.

*Ruth Berlau: photo taken by either
Brecht or Charles Laughton, 1944-45*

The cast of Galileo, *New York 1947*

Brecht and Ruth Berlau, 1944-45: photo taken
with Brecht's Leica, probably by Laughton

6

The Thornton Wilder Connection, 1946-1948. Wilder had spent time in Germany before 1933 and, according to Ruth Berlau, the ostensibly original production scheme of his play *Our Town* (1938) – actors breaking out of the story to talk to the audience, a stage only partially transformed into the illusion of a fictive place – was a 'steal' from Brecht. This is, of course, a gratuitous assumption since (a) the scheme could have been stolen from others, such as the Russians, and (b) it may not have been stolen at all. But the allegation is noteworthy as connected with the obsession which everyone in Brecht circles had with the Eminent, the Successful, in a word the Powerful. (Noteworthy also as reflecting Brecht's own paranoid suspicions. John Willett reports that as late as 1956, Brecht was accusing Wilder of 'pinching idea of [BB's only partially written novel about Julius Caesar], then writing offensive letter.' No such letter seems to have survived.)

Brecht would send Paul Dessau running to beg Stravinsky to make an opera from a Brecht libretto – and Dessau was a 'Brecht composer' who wished to do the job himself. Brecht tried hard to get a Big Name, preferably Archibald MacLeish, to accompany him to his confrontation with the Un-American Committee in 1947. And then there was Thornton Wilder. Brecht had been tipped off (by whom?) that Wilder was *the* big name who might be able to put over the BB plays in the USA. (Kurt Weill could help, W. H. Auden might be able to help, but Wilder could more than help, he could . . . he could . . .!) So in the winter of 1945-6 a meeting was arranged with the distinguished author of the possibly-plagiarized *Our Town.* Since nothing came of it, Brecht had me run after Wilder and tell him to translate *The Good Woman of Setzuan.* This is the answer Wilder sent me in a letter dated 3 July 1946:

When I met Mr Brecht last winter I told him of my admiration for *Der gute Mensch* and my hope of being able to translate it. I could not promise, though. I was just out of

32

the Army and could not foresee what projects of my own might take shape. After the shilly-shallying moods of re-adjustment I began to catch on to a subject and I returned the text with regret to Dr [Paul] Czinner and wrote a note to Mr Brecht saying that I could not undertake the work after all. There's one translation I've committed myself to, though, that'll interest you. I'd rather you didn't tell Mr Brecht, though, for it would appear to have been a choice made in values rather than one reflecting personal relations . . .

Wilder is referring to a Sartre play, and I think he did prefer Jean-Paul Sartre to Brecht, too, as did my friend the Nietzsche scholar Walter Kauffmann. Nor was Sartre the only one thus preferred. I received a postcard from Thornton Wilder in (?) 1948 which contained the following 'N.B.': 'Lorca may not be as influential as Brecht but he's better any day.' (Which, as I reported above, was what Eisler also had said. Was it a thought that haunted a whole generation?)

7

W. H. Auden 1947-48, 1953-54, 1959-60, 1964-65. Auden has been quoted saying that Brecht is a person one could easily imagine facing a death sentence and that he himself would enjoy being the executioner. Ruth Berlau, on the other hand, reporting Brecht's view of Auden is obviously aware only of very high esteem. What actually went on?

Auden often got the rough end of Brecht's stick and after his death received an even rougher end from the Heirs when they commissioned a *Mahagonny* translation from him without mentioning that they had Marc Blitzstein making another translation at the same time.

My own firsthand reporting, here, amounts only to a marginal note. The first bad treatment Auden received at Brecht's hands might have seemed my doing. Auden, with his friend Jimmy Stern, had translated *The Caucasian Chalk Circle*. As often Brecht expressed dissatisfaction with the result. Why didn't I try a version? 'Not unless Auden and Stern withdraw of their own free will', was my reply. 'Ask them to: they will,' said Brecht, so I wrote Stern. In a letter dated 9 December 1947, Stern replied: 'I did not know that I had "got across with Brecht". I'm sorry he didn't like my translation of the *Kreidekreis*. I'm sure he'll like yours better. I never could understand why you didn't do it in the first place. Betrayed? Good Lord, no. Not even surprised . . .'

Not even surprised. Stern had BB's number, and in a letter to me dated (?) 5 January 1948, Auden added: 'I have no contract with Brecht that would get in your way, and of course I have no objection to any negotiations you may make. Good luck with them. *You'll need it.*' The italics are mine, but the innuendo is all Auden's.

My next contact with him came in 1953 when Brecht said he would endorse my version of *Mother Courage* but that I should have Auden collaborate with me on the lyrics. No full-scale collaboration took place largely because Auden was fairly happy with *my* lyrics but he did send me the following advice from his lair on Ischia in a letter dated 31 October (?1953):

> The first thing to decide is whether we should try to make the translations fit the Dessau music or ignore the latter entirely. Personally, seeing that they are chants, not operatic song, i.e. the music is subordinate to the words, I am strongly in favour of the latter course, since it makes it infinitely easier to make a translation that is readable. However, you are the translator and must decide. If you want to keep the original music, there are one or two spots where your words don't fit, e.g. 'Lucky all mortals who have none' has the first accent in the wrong place. Let me know what you think.

Six years passed. In July 1959, I find myself writing Auden in his Tyrolean retreat of that time:

> You will recall that in 1953 you helped me with the lyrics from the play [*Mother Courage*] and expressed the thought that you might help me more later if necessary. Well, you seem to be the only person who would be accepted by both myself and the Brecht family as to what is a good script! . . . They would like to hear what you think of my script . . .

This elicited a cable from Kirchstetten, Austria, reading: 'Translation seems perfectly OK to me writing, Auden.'
I don't think Auden did 'write' anything further at that point but a little later on I find him offering assistance *in court* if I should have further difficulties with the Brecht Estate:

> The documents seem clear enough and, needless to say, Jimmy Stern or I would confirm our share of the proceedings in court, if your lawyers advise an action.

In 1964 the *Mother Courage* negotiation was resumed. The National Theatre (London) would do the play in my translation, but with 'lyrics by W. H. Auden'. The joke this time is that he had a secret collaborator – myself. For it happened that we were both artists-in-residence in Berlin for the winter of 1964-5, and so I was able to drive over and work with him any time he wanted . . .
This is all trivia. Less trivial is the contradiction existing between Brecht's desire to have Auden's name on the plays and the lack of real sympathy either for Auden's work or

persona. This I might have inferred quite early on from a brief exchange between Brecht and myself in Santa Monica that went something like this:

EB: Auden was brought up an Anglican.
BB: 'Church of England'?
EB: *High* Church – the closest to the church of Rome.
BB: Ah, yes! Isherwood says, 'Now there's nothing left but the height.'
EB: That was some years ago. He's re-converted now.
BB: Seriously? Oh, well, I could handle that. Do something for me. Bring Auden over some time. I can deprive him of those illusions in short order.
EB: In one meeting?
BB: In about twenty minutes, yes.

But if Brecht misunderstood Auden, Auden, I felt, returned the compliment, which feeling came through to me most strongly on an occasion when I asked Auden who would be the right American composer to provide the music for a Brecht play and Auden suggested Samuel Barber. Since I know that Auden fully appreciated the quality of Barber's style, I can only conclude that he was not really in touch with Brecht's. In this sense I can agree with the Russian dissident Joseph Brodsky, who thinks Auden should have had nothing to do with Brecht. (Brodsky's reasons are political, mine are aesthetic.)

Talking with Auden, I came to find his whole relation to *Deutschtum* profoundly ambiguous. His prejudice – pose, if you will – was anti-Gallic. Already before Hitler, it was Germany he went to, not France or Italy. But his Teutonicism was only skin-deep. I heard him – this must have been in 1964 or 1965 – lecture in German. He was fluent, even fast-speaking. But the grammar was all wrong. German is all a matter of word-endings, and Auden didn't care how any of their words ended: he knew the stems and talked on and on without a word of English, even invoking flourishes of German colloquialism . . .

8

Zurich, 1948. In the 1940s Brecht had two hair-breadth escapes. The first was in Moscow in 1941. Had he stayed a week longer, it seems likely that he would have disappeared into the Gulag, as his one-time girlfriend Carola Neher – the Polly of the *Threepenny Opera* film – had already done. (Tretyakov, his Russian champion and translator, was simply shot.) The second was in New York in 1947. Just before he left for Europe, the FBI decided to detain him in America for questioning. But instead of using the phone or Western Union, they sent the instructions from Washington to New York by mail. These arrived too late, and the bird had flown.

Financed by the Guggenheim Foundation, I followed in 1948. Let me try to re-capture several images.

One: Brecht in his new, temporary home near Zurich; his confrontation with the Un-American Activities Committee in Washington five thousand miles away. He has a small phonograph, and is playing a disc recording of that confrontation for Paul Dessau and me. When we've heard it out, he provides several extra details: that one of his lawyers had advised him to say he had been a card-carrying Party member, since otherwise the Committee would fault him by forging such a card; secondly, that he would have pleaded the First or Fifth Amendment but had been advised that, as a foreigner, he was not entitled to, so instead he declared that, no, no, no, he had never been a Communist; and thirdly, that the Americans weren't as bad as the Nazis because they let a man smoke even during a grilling, and that this enabled him to pause and think out his answers between inhalations.

Two: Same location, one day later. Enter Dessau with music MS on which he has written the music for the Song of the Water Seller in *The Good Woman of Setzuan*. When Dessau sings and plays for us at the upright piano, and I praise the music, Brecht says: 'It's good but it's not right, it's opera, it's concert music, it's not a work song.' His words bring him to his feet, he starts to indicate (not fully embody) the role of

37

Wang, makes us imagine a pole across his shoulder, and begins to speak-sing. He does not sing Dessau's tune, or any tune, but croaks out a rhythmic pattern – if there's a tune it is one the composer won't remember. He'll remember the rhythmic pattern, which will bring to his composer's mind the appropriate melody. I know this because another image I retain is that of Dessau coming in next day with a big smile on his face. 'Is this it?' He plays and sings. It is Brecht's performance *plus a tune*. Brecht, acknowledging a bull's eye, laughs with pleasure. I think to myself: 'Then maybe he did write the tune of Mack the Knife as I've heard him hint that he did!' Dessau has made himself into Brecht, I also think, as I observe that he's copied BB's Roman hair-do and his clothes (grey workshirt etc.).

Three: Brecht in the small picturesque commuter train between his pretty suburb of Feldmeilen and downtown Zurich. He doesn't approve of Switzerland, so Ruth has told me, because the Swiss workers are happy – when would they ever rebel? And he dislikes the picturesque in general, which in itself is to dislike Switzerland. Eisler even told me Brecht hated Beethoven because of the hieratic stance, the sacred holier-than-God sound. *Violins in themsleves bothered him*: my theory on this was that he could never get out of his head the story of Lenin listening to Beethoven's Appassionata Sonata and declaring music *too* beautiful because it tempts you into stroking your brother's head and forgetting that he'll bite your hand off. And so it is that Brecht detaches himself from Switzerland even more decisively than he had from America when he lived there. Yes, on the Swiss train he is even more absent than on the IRT. And where does the fantasy of the great realist wander off to? Where but Mother Russia, though the script in his hands, and from which he reads to me on the train (less noisy than the IRT), is ostensibly Greek: his *Antigone*. What he's reading is the narrative of an invader's disastrous, bloody defeat. At the end, he looks up from the page to say with flashing eyes: 'Stalingrad!'

A fourth image: Brecht at the movies in Zurich. Ruth has arranged for the three of us to see a film we are all familiar with: *The Gold Rush*. Brecht was big on happiness, friendly to hedonism, especially in his youth, but – by that token, maybe – was far from the happiest of men. He was not neurotically unable to relish the elementary pleasures: eating, drinking, sex, but the World (as seen very politically) was too much with him and made him, in his own words, lose his enthusiasm for love-making, while even eating seemed something squeezed in between battles. Sometimes, surely, he must have made love *with* enthusiasm? I have certainly – in Zurich and elsewhere – seen him eat and drink at leisure and with ample enjoyment. Never did I witness him having a better time that at *The Gold Rush* in Zurich. He was murmuring and gurgling with relish even when not laughing out loud. A specially memorable moment came when Chaplin disposed of the villain in the film by having an avalanche descend on him: in a trice he has fallen into an abyss. Brecht laughed, poked me in the ribs, and whispered: 'Our playwrights would have taken twenty minutes to get rid of the man!' I rather think there is more theatre wisdom in this off-the-cuff comment than in any hundred pages of his abstract theorizing and programizing.

There was another good Brechtian moment – Image Five – that afternoon at the movies. There were newsreels in those days, followed by some cute little feature story or turn. Today the feature was a performer who could balance a pile of cups on his head. And even a few on his chin! Brecht loved all that with the love of a six-year-old child, and, when the over-serious Professor Bentley hinted that, still, this was trivial and useless stuff for us realists and reformers, Brecht was quite firm in his defence of art for art's sake. 'You see,' he explained afterwards with smiles and much animation, 'more is more. If you can add something to life, *anything*, that's good! Who cares if it's just a *small* addition! That man added!' (Hanns Eisler used to say that the *Gebrauchskunst* – functional art – of radio commercials in America made him long for a country dedicated to art for art's sake.)

Brecht and Bentley outside the Schauspielhaus,
Zurich 1948 (photo: Ruth Berlau)

Brecht and Bentley, Zurich 1948
(photo: Ruth Berlau)

Bentley directing Kenneth Tynan
in Him, *Salzburg 1950*

9

Brecht the Bad Correspondent. In his lifetime Brecht was the man who never answered letters. We know now that he answered all the letters he wanted to answer. I for one should have realized this at the outset, and let him ignore letters he wished to ignore. Instead I made myself a nuisance by pestering him with demands for replies. Thus it is that the first sentence of his first letter to me (1945) reads: '*Sie haben ja ein abscheuliches Temperament*' – 'you certainly have a frightful temperament.' Later he had kinder if not truer things to say of me. And he told this anecdote:

> One day a man came into a cigar store and said to the owner: 'give me a cigar'. The owner was speechless, but laughed and handed over the cigar. Next day the man came again and again said: 'give me a cigar'. This time the owner hesitated but then handed over the cigar. But when the man came yet again on the third day and asked for a cigar, the owner was ready for him and stood firm. 'Please!' said the man. 'But can you give me a reason why I *should* give you a cigar?' asked the owner. 'Certainly,' said the man: 'I'm the man you give a cigar to every day.'

10

Austrian intermezzo, 1949-50. The residency which BB took up – now a world-historical fact – was Berlin but the citizenship he acquired – not without some brouhaha in the world press – was Austrian. He proposed to play a role in the Salzburg Festivals, and was in and out of Salzburg in years when I happened to be in and out of Salzburg in a different connection indeed, a connection with the Salzburg Seminar which had recently been set up by some Harvard students at Schloss Leopoldskron. Were the two of us a living example of détente? The Seminars were certainly part of the apparatus of the new American imperialism – a liberal part, by all means – and we only narrowly and accidentally missed getting BB to the Schloss as a distinguished speaker. Brecht in this period was effectively entering the service of the new Russian imperialism – 'socialism' imposed on non-Russian territory by the Red Army – but there was no wall as yet in Berlin, and Brecht was continually issuing invitations to such as myself to be his guests in the East. I was present at the moment at some social gathering in Salzburg when he conceived – improvised in conversation – his proferred Austrian play, a *Salzburg Dance of Death* never to be completed, in some words such as these:

> Rich people cannot understand why they die; it seems so unfair. So they go to Death and say: 'Couldn't something be worked out? Surely there are enough *poor* people to keep you busy?' Death says all right so long as they make it clear to him, when he approaches on professional business, which *are* the rich ones. A sign is agreed on, and for a while the new system works well. The poor die and the rich bid fair to be immortal. But the latter have overlooked one small point: Death has a bad memory. How should he not have? There are so many poor people who have to die. And now, watching out for a sign given by the rich takes up time and attention. Death does not manage to maintain the efficiency of the early days of his compact. One day he lets a rich man

die. Receiving the indignant protests of the still-living rich, he makes a slight effort. It is no good. He is on the downward path, and soon is as indiscriminate as in the past. You can't make deals with Death.

Since the critic Kenneth Tynan later became Brecht's chief champion in London, it is pertinent to mention that he and I worked together in Salzburg, June, 1950. I directed e. e. cummings' *Him*; Ken played the title role. What principally came of the collaboration was not a good production. I didn't believe in the play strongly enough to do it justice, and Ken at the time was busy reaching the conclusion that he was not an actor. What came of the collaboration was conversation. 'Who *is* this Bertolt Brecht?' was the question on Ken's mind, and I dealt with it – at least to the point of arousing enough curiosity to lead to further developments.

The next contact between us was when he arranged for the National Theatre to stage my version of *Mother Courage* in 1965.

The people responsible for Mother Courage*:*
Erich Engel (director), Brecht (author), Paul Dessau
(Composer), Helene Weigel (actress)

Brecht's production of Mother Courage *at the Munich Kammerspiele, 1950, designed by Teo Otto. Erni Wilhelms (Kathrin); Therese Giehse (Courage); Hans Christian Blech (Eilif) and Karl Lieffer (Schoerzerkas). (Photo: Hildegard Steinmetz)*

11

Berlin, 1949-50. It was not just in Salzburg but also in Berlin that Brecht was cast in the role of Mr East, and I in that of Mr West. In 1949 the Soviet Union tried to isolate Berlin by blockade but the United States defeated this intention by flying supplies in from Frankfurt. I was one of the supplies. I got to Berlin by special permit on a US army plane, and my mission for 'the West' was to give some talks in the western sectors of Berlin and meet with the cultural officers in the US military government. An incidental observation I made was that the same US army which on principle excluded homosexuals had actually let quite a few in and was now hunting them up so they could be 'Cultural Officers' and run the culture of occupied Germany. Everyone knows that to-be-gay-is-to-be-sissy-is-to-be-cultured, and perhaps this is where Gay Liberation really started. One of these officers told me that when he'd been asked: are you bi-zonal? he'd replied: no, just bisexual, and his superior officers thought it a wonderful joke. . . .

Despite the blockade, things could be more relaxed in those days than they became later: there was, for instance, no difficulty in phoning the East from the West in Berlin. Nor did the American authorities seem to hold it against me when the first thing I did in West Berlin was ask the way to East Berlin.

Brecht and Weigel both seemed welcome to the higher-ups in the US military government. 'Budd Schulberg's brother is going to show us Hitler's film about the 1944 officers' plot,' Ruth Berlau announced. That was at the HQ of military government in Dahlem, and I recall that Weigel was delighted to receive foodstuffs from the PX provided by Schulberg and his friends. (Monster ingratitude! A little later on, Brecht and Dessau would write a song representing those who had received food packages from America as traitors.)

11 January 1949: a landmark in theatre history – Mother Courage *opens in East Berlin*. The special permit had not arrived in time for me to attend but I made it to a performance soon thereafter and it was a landmark in my life. Many details are clear in memory after thirty-five years including surrounding circumstances. The Berlin subway was totally unlit at the time of the blockade, both the trains and the stations, and one could only find out where one was by asking some passenger who was familiar with the territory. The city had not yet been rebuilt after the bombings, so one went to see *Mother Courage* in terrain reminiscent of the Thirty Years' War, all ruin and rubble. Walking from the Friedrichstrasse station to the theatre, one shuddered a little passing the windowless building which the Russians were using as a prison. Brecht hadn't been sure I'd make it to the theatre that night and indeed it was curtain time when I arrived and every seat in the house was occupied. However, he had gone to the trouble of waiting for me in the lobby. Muttering '*Pünktlich, pünktlich!*' – punctual, punctual!' – he grabbed a chair and pushed both me and it into a side box just above the stage. . . .

When the curtain came down on this wondrous piece of modern theatre, Brecht had left, so I went to Weigel's dressing-room and later walked her home, 'home' at the time being the Hotel Adlon. Another Brechtian situation! The Adlon had been the Waldorf Astoria of Berlin. Now most of it was rubble but a surviving section housed the Brechts, and housed them in the Brechtian lifestyle: a big room for Weigel and Brecht here, and just down the hall, Ruth Berlau's smaller room.

I already knew most of the Ruth Berlau story as it has since been publicly told in James Lyon's *Brecht in America* and elsewhere – the baby boy she'd had by Brecht, his death, her committal to Bellevue by Brecht – but Ruth didn't know I knew, and in the American years did not confide in me. However, on this visit to Berlin, I learned from Ruth of Weigel's jealousy. Brecht would go on the assumption that, since Marxists despise jealousy, they are not jealous. Ruth knew better. She knew Brecht himself was the most jealous of men. For that matter *she* was jealous of Weigel; but she held her own. 'Why, Weigel doesn't even know his favourite brand of cigars!' she protested, while admitting that this ignorance provided the opportunity for her knowledge, for her kind of caring. 'I like your ring, Ruth,' I said one day on this trip. 'It's from Brecht,' she said. 'Is it silver?' I asked. 'Oh yes,' she explained, 'you know: gold for marriage, silver for love.'

En route for the Adlon, I reported to Weigel that everyone, including myself, had been in tears during her final scene. 'Is this all right in a play by Bertolt Brecht?' 'Maybe,' she said with a satisfied smile that actually read, 'certainly, and I love it.' On the other hand, she was pleased to be able to give a 'Brechtian' account of the means by which a supreme emotional effect had been achieved. In the same final sequence in which Courage goes out alone into what seems an endless night, her cheeks were hollow, as if she'd lost ten pounds since the scene before. 'How do you do that?' 'Shall I tell you my secret?' 'Definitely!' 'I remove my dentures. And there's nowhere on stage to put them, so I hold them in my hand till just before the curtain call.'

The 'silent scream' Weigel emitted after she had pretended not to recognize the corpse of her son had not been 'discovered' yet when I saw the play. It *was* a discovery, not something thought out. 'One night,' I heard her tell later, 'no sound came out, it was as simple as that. After the show I got compliments on this "idea". I kept it in, so now it *is* an "idea".'

I don't know if Brecht wanted the public to know Weigel took her dentures out, but he did want them to know how such things as silent screams come about. He told this story about Peter Lorre in *A Man's a Man*, 1931. Lorre was told to turn pale on stage. When he asked how an actor could possibly do such a thing on command, Brecht said: 'Have some white paint ready in a bowl upstage, then turn away from the audience and smear your face with the paint. When you turn around, they'll see you've also turned pale.'

Again, I don't know if BB wanted either the public or the critics to take up just those matters but he did want the critics to describe more, and judge less. 'What they say about my plays doesn't matter, my plays will survive the critics, but what they say about my productions matters very much because what they write is all that posterity will know of the subject.'

It was during this Berlin visit that Ruth took me to a meeting of the Communist Youth, euphemistically called the Freie Deutsche Jugend, where Brecht was going to talk and be talked to. Many of the kids seemed willing to let Brecht explain things to them – his play or the world – but breathing hotly down his neck were the zealots. The play was just anti-war, pacifistic, wasn't it? Well, Brecht said, picking his words carefully, it presented *a* war, and that war was a wholly bad one with the people on both sides the losers. But what then does your play do, the zealots countered, for our heroes, fighting for socialism in wars of national liberation? The voices asking the questions are excited but the playwright resorts to his own alienation effect, cooling what might have been a shouting match into a scene from his treatise-in-dialogue-form *Messingkauf*: 'There was, of course, no socialism in the seventeenth century.'

The zealots no doubt were all set to ask why he had to write about the seventeenth century when Brecht cleverly interrupted to ask if anything in the form of his play had caught their attention. Oh yes, the form was quite strange and in places perverse. How can you stop the story to have Eilif sing and perform a sword dance? Brecht took the kind of pause he had made famous before the Un-American Committee in Washington: giving himself time to think while taking a long slow puff at his cigar. 'Two answers to your question. First, there are places and times where and when people do such a song and dance. Second (and this with a slight smile): *warum nicht*? – why not?'

The 'free' German youth of 1949 had spent their infancy under Hitler and were now spending their adolescence under Stalin and Ulbricht. Ruth took me to a session Brecht had one day with professional acting students. He had a question for them. Why this profession and not another? What made them want to be – of all things – actors? Many of the answers came close to a statement James Dean made a few years later to the effect that acting, for him, had to do with being neurotic: not that it necessarily proved to be a cure, a therapy, rather it was the way one's neurosis expressed itself, worked itself out. 'You're all Americans!' Brecht said with a laugh. 'This is exactly what I used to hear at the Actors' Lab in Hollywood!' 'Well, Herr Brecht,' said one bold soul, 'what would you have liked us to say?' 'There are more good answers than one,' Brecht replied, 'but there *was* one I heard not long ago that I especially liked. It's Charles Laughton's answer: "I like to imitate great men".'

Another question: 'I'm asking you to play a Berlin police-man. How will you go about it?' Here a boy who had some Stanislavsky-type training in Weimar made a speech about tell-ing himself he *is* a policeman until he *becomes* one by (though this was not his language) sheer intensity of identification. There followed some discussion of the psychology of acting, the conclusion another calculated interruption by Brecht: 'No one has suggested going out on the street and watching policemen. Listening to them. What about *observation* as an actor's first task? No introspection: one's insides are invisible except by X-ray. Observation of *others*.' 'But Herr Brecht,' says a timid voice, 'just imitating, copying, isn't that going to be too flat, literal, naturalistic?' Brecht's voice gets much louder. '*Nein*! No! Who has acted policemen best?' (Silence.) 'Oh come on, *you* know! Even if he *was* banned under Hitler, banned for *playing* Hitler – Yes, exactly, Charlie Chaplin. Or what about the Keystone Kops?'

Of course, these students had already done some homework on Brecht and had questions for *him*. 'We've read about Epic Theatre, the Alienation Effect, well, the new kind of acting you ask for, has it ever happened, did anyone ever get it right, have any of your plays ever been acted in that completely new way?' 'Well, I've seen The Thing Happen at moments and, wait a minute, there was one whole performance that had It. When we were rehearsing my *Round Heads and Pointed Heads* in Copenhagen, the Nazi Embassy put pressure on the Danes and the play was banned. However, we learned we could legally present a rehearsal – just not a finished performance. How could we make a legally clear distinction between a rehearsal and a performance?' "Hm," said one actor, "in a performance you don't have a script in your hand: if you have a script in your hand, that makes it a rehearsal." Actually, the actors had memorized their lines, but I sent them on stage that night with scripts in their hands. These scripts got in the way of the action – constructively! Broke up the smooth lines. Came between the lover and the shoulders he needed two hands to embrace. In other words brought about the Alienation Effect, provided a more complex contour for the composition, added style.' 'And on subsequent evenings, Herr Brecht?' 'Unfortunately, the actors learned to take the scripts in stride. Smoothed everything out. Returned to the performance they had been giving before the ban . . . Such was my one evening of Epic Theatre!'

Mother Courage established the Berlin Ensemble as the great theatre company of our time, and early in 1950 *The Private Tutor* proved that the art of Brecht, Weigel, Busch, Neher et al. could be handed on to the younger generation. It was a production without the oldsters, without 'stars'; but *all* the young people in it seemed to be stars. That was the achievement, and in retrospect it seems amazing that the Ensemble reached its peak so quickly. I would see the Company again in 1956, 1960, 1964-5, and 1967. It was always good, and probably the best in the world, but 1950 remains the *annus mirabilis*. Even the sardonic Brecht was euphoric that year. Delighted with my delight over *The Private Tutor*, he bubbled over: 'Write me a telegram in English to send to Hambleton!' (This was the American producer of his *Galileo*.)

'Saying what?' '*Private Tutor* something you must produce in America. Come at once!'

It must have been about that time, too, that Brecht told me he had at last and definitely inherited the crown. When I asked what crown that was, he explained that the German theatre always had a king. In his youth, it was Gerhart Hauptmann, in his early maturity it was Georg Kaiser, now it was himself.

Hambleton did not come, at once or otherwise, nor would anyone else from the professional American theatre. As late as 1954 I offered *Mother Courage* to Lawrence Langner of the Theatre Guild, suggesting that he might try it out modestly at his summer theatre in Westport, Connecticut. He replied:

Dear Eric, OLD [sic!] MOTHER COURAGE is a wonderful play but too misery for the good old summertime as well as the good old winter time, so am returning same . . .

At that, he must be given higher marks than my own New York agent whose only comment, on reading the same masterpiece, was 'is this supposed to be a play?'

My relationship with Brecht also reached a peak in 1950; and then fell. The pains of the later process were no less because the problems were professional and political rather than personal. A main cause of trouble was an article I had brought out in *Theatre Arts* magazine, late in 1949, about the first half of the twentieth century in theatre. For while I attributed to Brecht an importance ('the most original dramatist now writing') the world had not yet conceded him, I also stated that his mind was in bondage to Soviet Communism. The way Ruth Berlau was to put it was: 'You said Brecht would be a better writer if he were not a Communist: you're crazy!' But this is to anticipate.

The Kammerspiele, 8 October 1950: Mother Courage *opens in Munich*. In Italy during the summer I'd heard that Brecht would go to Munich in the fall to direct *Mother Courage* at the Kammerspiele. Unable to reach him beforehand, I drove north, turned up early at the first rehearsal, and sat in one of the directorial chairs on stage. When Brecht arrived he took in the situation at a glance and grinned: '*Der Bentley natürlich, pünktlich wie immer!*' – 'It's Bentley of course, punctual as ever!' After rehearsal he asked the Kammerspiele people to hire me as an assistant. They declined but I took the position, anyway, without salary – alongside the two paid assistants, Ruth Berlau and Egon Monk, the latter a young director from the Berlin Ensemble (later director of very fine TV presentations, shown on public TV in America, such as *One Day* and *The Oppermanns*). This meant that I not only attended all rehearsals but that I met with Brecht and the two other assistants most evenings in his hotel room. For two or three hours we would discuss the day's rehearsal – its pluses, its minuses, the conclusions we should draw, the action we would plan for the day following. I came to regard such meetings as central to the production process, and wished later I could have persuaded American colleagues to hold them.

There were fringe benefits also to my presence in the hotel room. I would be present when journalists interviewed Brecht, and he would always say, as I offered to leave, 'No, no, stay, we may need your collaboration.' A literary moment comes to mind. A journalist was telling Brecht that Marcel Proust was the great French novelist of the century. As imperturbably as he had announced the superiority of Eisler to Schoenberg, Brecht admonished his interviewer: 'Well, no; for us, Anatole France is more important.'

On the whole, the Munich production of *Courage* could be deemed as dazzling, as moving, as much fun as the Berlin production. Built like a washerwoman, and seeming to belong utterly to the workaday and desperate world of

Mother Courage, Therese Giehse in the title role might be considered less Brechtian than Weigel in that she did not comment from outside but got thoroughly inside the role, Stanislavsky-fashion. But I thought she was ideal.

I was now anxious not only to translate but direct the Brecht plays. To be sitting in Brecht's rehearsals and evening staff-meetings during those autumnal weeks would be my chance to see exactly how he did things. He was the quietest director I've ever seen at work. Some people said he was *too* quiet and didn't intervene enough; but this was an illusion. He felt that a flow, a continuum, was needed to get the actors' creative juices working. Energy had to be generated or 'nothing would happen', and it is the aim of directing to cause 'things' to 'happen'. Quietness can help and is not just an abstention. The actors (I am close to quoting Brecht's own words here, also Ruth Berlau's when she was quoting him) must sense that the silent director is on the edge of his seat paying attention: they must feel watched, listened to, appreciated. In the comic passages, Brecht's silence would be punctuated by very quick and spontaneous laughter. This might tell an actor that a passage he had supposed humdrum was in fact hilarious. Or it might express appreciation of his talent. Either way it was economical and unobtrusive directing.

'You must know,' Brecht would tell us would-be directors, 'how to go with the flow when you interrupt; never interrupt when it would stop the flow. Save comment for later.' In other words, he realized, as much as Stanislavsky, that it's the actor who creates the living performance. Much as Brecht admired Meyerhold, he would never have said, as Meyerhold is supposed to have said to an actor: 'You roll up into a ball: I'll throw you.'

Naturalism was a bad word in Brecht's vocabulary yet I think it must be applied to his voice work with actors. Many of the German actors made all plays sound grandly declamatory, like Schiller. Brecht wanted, on the contrary, to sound down-to-earth like Büchner. So when they made his lines sound like Schiller, he would send them out with Egon Monk and me for coaching in the desired kind of speech. We had to completely change their speech melody. If an actor had a long speech, we would break it down into short units that could be treated as quick remarks in a present day conversation. 'How would you say that, talking with me now, or to your wife at breakfast?' With some difficulty, the actor would find what ought to have been the easier – the more natural – way of phrasing and intonation. This was Brecht's answer to *Wallenstein*.

If Brecht fired actors, it would usually be because they were too noble. In Zurich, the unfavourite actor of both Brecht and Weigel had been Will Quadfleig, a 'noble' Hamlet, Brecht's ideal casting for Hamlet being Peter Lorre: 'Shakespeare himself says Hamlet was fat.' Two actors were fired during the *Courage* rehearsals in Munich. One was a girl with a beautiful soprano voice. '*Too* beautiful,' said Brecht, 'the stage becomes a concert platform when she sings. Also, she's only giving us notes, bypassing the words which don't express beauty but complacency to an almost insolent degree. We need an actress who can play the complacency, the insolence.' We got one. Her soprano was not super-fine but this pleased Brecht. 'Not a singer performing in a hall, a girl singing in a kitchen.' The other actor to be fired was a young man who played the angry soldier in scene four (the capitulation scene). He wanted the scene to generate anger as it went along, but what Brecht had written was someone already in a towering rage when the scene begins. This gives the actor a harder assignment and probably seemed to him the wrong way to write a scene: he expected to be given the opportunity to work up anger. That is what Brecht called 'the old theatre'. The 'new theatre', like Chaplin, prefers to plunge *in medias res*. Then again, our young man simulated strong emotion by merely increasing the decibels. 'You shout so loud I can't hear you,' said Brecht. Effects which the 'old theatre' got with shouts, Brecht got by mutterings and whispers.

If the vocal work could be called naturalistic, the 'blocking' could be called stylized, almost mannered, definitely pictorial and formal. Brecht would go through a scene like a movie director noting every 'frame' in a sequence. Every 'frame' had to please him as a piece of visual art, and, once the show was running through without a break, he had Ruth make still photographs every few seconds. (The click of her camera had driven Charles Laughton to threaten to kill her with his bare hands if she didn't stop.)

When I say 'almost mannered', I have in mind groupings and movements of Brecht's which he seemed to introduce as often as possible in all his plays. His pet hate was actors in a straight line or symmetrically disposed across the stage. His preference was, for example, a solitary figure in one corner, and a clump of figures at a distance (a clump, not a row). As to movement, he had been struck, when young, by the way Frank Wedekind (after whom Brecht named his elder son) would walk straight

54

across the stage close to the footlights. To the end Brecht would have two things to say about actors' 'walks': first, don't walk a pace or two, make it a walk clear across the stage; second, don't walk while talking, or even while someone else is talking, walk in silence, make a dramatic pause out of your walk, let the only sound be the sound of your feet. Here Brecht the director was carrying out the plans of Brecht the dramatist: these 'walks' are not mere movements, are in no way decorative, but are action, and action powered by some high dynamic such as aggression or anger.

He would not always claim to know in advance what move was best – or whether movement was needed. Even though he'd written the script, he was not one of those directors who work out all the movement in their heads beforehand. At the end of the capitulation scene, Mother Courage, he said, might walk off, or she might just stand there. There were these alternatives, and indeed several others, and he put Frau Giehse through her paces trying out half a dozen ways of ending the little scene. A whole morning was spent on this: getting her up, sitting her down, changing the cues on which she does this or that. An American director would undoubtedly have consulted *her* along the way. Brecht was the European dictator-direct in that he didn't consult actors. Frau Giehse was of course free to tell him anything that was on her mind at lunch afterwards, but he did not allow discussion during rehearsal. (It was at lunch that I asked Frau Giehse if she always allowed her director to push her around as Brecht had done in preparing the end of the capitulation scene. 'Only if he's a genius,' she replied.) If an actor wanted to try out an idea, he could say so before the rehearsal started, and Brecht would say: 'Don't explain, don't justify, but by all means show me. Show me right now.' And he was often happy to accept an idea that was entirely the actor's own. The actor playing the Dutch Cook in Munich thought the man would be more interesting if he didn't just have a Dutch accent but gave the impression of thinking in Dutch and only translating into German. He took lessons in Dutch so he could find the Dutch words for the German speeches in Brecht's script. *Something was added* to the role, and Brecht was delighted.

What that actor did enriched the comic texture of *Mother Courage*, the significant premise being that the highly uncomical tale does have a comic texture. In conversation Brecht took no umbrage at my notion that his Epic Theatre, untraditional as it might claim to be in relation to tragedy, was in the tradition of comic theatre. Brecht was not only witty in himself but was never happier than when teaching young actors to be witty. To an actor who kept laughing, presumably hoping to get the audience to laugh with him: 'The more laughter on stage, the less out front.' To an actress who got the giggles while rehearsing: 'A —, if it's really that funny, you should pay the price of admission.' An American visitor, hoping to be associated with a Broadway production of *Mother Courage*, asked Brecht if he had advice for the American actors. Answer: 'Tell them to play the comedy – the tragic elements, the ideas, all that will take care of itself.'

The American visitor was Edward F. Kook, president of the lighting company that supplied all the Broadway theatres with their lighting equipment. Before going to Germany, he had read me to the effect that Brecht used white light only. 'It can't be true,' Kook said, 'you just don't know lighting. I'm going to Germany to see what they actually do.' He went, and I received an airmail postcard from him that read: 'You are ninety-nine per cent right.' Back in America, he told me the one per cent was steel blue, which of course is as near to white as you can get without being white . . .

Brecht's banishment of coloured light from the theatre certainly required explanation and of course received it from the Meister himself in his theoretical essays: the theatre should reveal, not conceal, illuminate, not leave in obscurity, demonstrate openly, not beat about the bush, etcetera etcetera. His old friend Caspar Neher had another explanation. After World War I, in the inflation period, power shortages were rife, and radically affected the theatre. Should they shut down? Revert to candles, gas, or arc lamps? Well, the more affluent theatre people had cars, and the big sporty cars of the era had external headlights, rather easily detached. Neher invented 'Brecht lighting' by detaching headlights and using them as stage floodlights. This lighting was (a) white and (b) very intense. (a) plus (b) equals BB lighting.

The Good Woman of Setzuan, *New York 1956: Uta Hagen,*
Zero Mostel, Nancy Marchand (photo: Fred Fehl)

Bentley's production of The Caucasian
Chalk Circle, *Philadelphia 1948*

Teo Otto's design for the final scene of The Good Woman of Setzuan, *used in Bentley's 1956 New York production*

Hanns Eisler, Harry Buckwitz and Teo Otto, Frankfurt [1956?]

13

Teo Otto in Munich – and After. 'Die Wahrheit ist konkret', it was Brecht's pleasure to declare, 'truth is concrete'. Certainly his own abstract ideas were mostly attempts to universalize the practice of certain individuals: the acting of Frank Wedekind, Albert Steinrück, Karl Vallentin, Helene Weigel, and Peter Lorre, the stage- and costume-designs of Casper Neher and . . . Teo Otto.

Brecht was the first to concede that it was Otto who found the way to stage *Mother Courage* and especially how to present the wagon, namely, on a turntable revolving in the opposite direction – opposite, that is, to the wagon's wheels. A notion simple to the point of näiveté in terms of mechanics, yet in terms of effect in a theatre, sensational! Teo Otto designed the Munich production; and I enjoyed bettering a friendly acquaintance made in Zurich in '49. He, Ruth, Dessau and the Viertels, were the only ones in 'the gang' with whom I ever got on first name (Du) terms.

Let me mention two of the many things I learned from Teo Otto. First: have the scenery ready at a much earlier point in rehearsals than is the custom in London and New York – the costumes even earlier so that the actors can rehearse in them for weeks. Second: don't design the costumes on reading the script but wait till you see the actors. Design your costumes for those particular bodies, those specific personalities. Draw the actors before making any other sketches. Then draw clothes on the actors you have drawn. This way they will *be* clothes, and not traditional 'theatre costumes' – such is Brechtian Realism. For BB and his collaborators abolished the costume play in the very act of re-creating the history play. Backstage a whole technique was worked out for making the scenery look old and the clothes look worn, a technique that had begun, perhaps, in 1928 with the ironing of grease into the pants for the *Threepenny Opera* . . .

Of Brecht's own clothes, my colleague John Fuegi likes to say: 'he would spare no expense to look poor', and the principle applies to the Brecht-Otto stage. No painted canvas, no three-ply wood or the like. For their *Mother Courage* , the Bavarians went out and chopped down forests, then 'spoiled' this superb new wood with a blow-torch to make it look old and worn. Ruined post-war Munich could afford what Broadway never in this world could have even considered.

In awestruck tones, since she was a good *bourgeoise* herself, Ruth confided to me: 'Teo is a *real* proletarian!' (The rest of us were fake proletarians.) Luckily, Otto didn't play the role assigned: real proletarians love bourgeois comfort and bourgeois culture when they can get them and Otto could get them, *had* got them. Outside of his superb talent, his main quality was gentleness. Second only to Ruth he was the warmest person in that entourage and second to none he was the gentlest. So I had to feel guilty later when I found out that he had got on Helene Weigel's enemies' list as a result of his loyalty to the friendship formed with me in Zurich and Munich 1949-50. This is what he wrote me several years after Brecht's death:

Lieber Eric Bentley . . . habe auch wenig Freunde in Ost und West – das macht nichts . . . da ich die Kampagne gegen Dich als Übersetzer und Antipoden von Steff nicht mitmachte, habe ich den Kontakt mit Helli verloren. Man verlangte, ich sollte mich gegen Dich erklären aber wie gesagt ich habe das abgelehnt. Hab eine schöne Zeit. Wir hören von einander. Dein, Teo Otto

Dear Eric Bentley . . . also I have very few friends either East or West – it makes no difference . . . Because I did not join the campaign against you as translator and as antipode of Steff [Stefan Brecht] I have lost contact with Helli [Helene Weigel]. It was demanded of me that I declare myself against you but, as I say, I refused. Have a lovely time. Let's hear from each other. Yours, Teo Otto

Teo was a man of the Old (pre-1933) Left. Tired and disappointed now, his position, finally, was not too far from that of Caspar Neher, who, sharing none of Brecht's political enthusiasms, had, during the Third Reich, simply kept as low a profile as possible. '*Die Politik ist eine Hure*', he informed me, 'politics is a whore.'

14

Again, Munich, Autumn 1950: a Restaurant (Name Forgotten).
I've said Brecht was a quiet director. He was so confidently so
that he allowed visitors in at any and all rehearsals, which is in
strong contrast to most American directors who either think
rehearsals are a great big secret and/or are afraid that they'll
be caught out throwing a tantrum. I've also said that Brecht
himself was given to the occasional tantrum. At which time he
would give what I used to call his Hitler imitation – screeching
till his voice broke! And it is in the logic of history that he
would find more 'Nazis' in Munich than he had in New York.

But he 'found' them too easily. He sat there 'finding'
them with two scientific instruments: the light meter and
the stop-watch. The light meter was in his hands so he could
check that 'they' gave him enough light on the stage. He would
run up on the stage, light meter in hand, to demonstrate that
'they' had not given him the intensity of white light that he
had demanded. 'But that's all we have, that's the maximum!'
'Then increase the maximum! Go out and buy more powerful
bulbs!'

The stop-watch was supposed to solve one of the main
technical problems of *Mother Courage*: long pauses between
the scenes. Each scene change had to take place in that number
of seconds which BB would allow. When his stop-watch told
him 'they' were taking more seconds than that, he would
have a fit. He would demand that the stage manager be
brought out on stage and then he would bawl him out in
language both harsh and raunchy. Having some acquaintance
with American workers, I was surprised that a stage manager
would take it – with fifty to a hundred invited guests in the
orchestra! This stage manager not only did so but accepted an
order from Brecht which in America would simply have been
disobeyed. Brecht told him to do the whole scene change again.
This entailed taking off stage everything his men had just put
on, putting back what was on before that, and then restoring
what was on in the first place. All this was done and, I assume,

in something like the time the stop-watch dictated for Brecht grunted and let the performance continue . . .

During the lunch break, he would take a twenty minute nap in a little room in the theatre set aside for the purpose. One day, however, he came galloping down the stairs, roaring that they had locked him out, they, of course, being the Munich *Scheisskerle* (shitheads), the NAZIS! Ruth whispered in my ear that she was going to run upstairs and check this out. In a minute, she returned and whispered something in Brecht's ear. For a split second he was in shock. Then he slunk back upstairs. What she had told him was that he'd made a mistake and tried the wrong door.

Still Munich is (not just was) the home of Nazism, and we encountered the real thing during an otherwise delightful *Oktoberfest* – an annual event in the city with much Bock beer and Wurst and, even in 1950, the kind of side show which had aroused BB's interest in 'another kind of acting' some thirty years earlier. Brecht and Ruth and I were in a tent having a couple of those beers when students at a nearby table started singing traditional German 'student tunes'. I say 'tunes' because I wasn't catching any of the words till I saw the face of Brecht turn purple. And then I thought Ruth and I were going to have a case of apoplexy on our hands. Suddenly, though, he got up. Ruth and I rose with him. Brecht kicked over the bench we'd all three been sitting on and stalked out. We followed. '*Genug! Das ist genug!*' – 'Enough! That's enough!' The song he'd walked out on had been about the '*Saujud,*' 'Jewish swine'[4]; and indeed it proved that we had been hearing several anti-Semitic compositions, one after the other. When we had put some distance between us and the Aryan swine, and were again seated, Brecht's voice carried an incredible intensity of feeling. No 'alienation' now. He looked me in the eye and said savagely: 'And they say these people have changed! Good liberals now, are they? I know this sort! They will never change! And in the East, they know this. Over there these hoodlums would be behind barbed wire! And never, never would they be let out.'

The thought that the Nazis were in our midst, and that we were in the midst of Nazis, remained with us throughout out stay in Munich, and at a late rehearsal Ruth asked that Frau Giehse, as Courage, jump, as it were, out of her role and 'point her finger at the Nazis in the audience'. This was to be when she sang:

War's just a business proposition
But not with cheese, with steel instead!

Only when I remarked that this would damage his play,
since anti-war propaganda was not in the character of Mother
Courage, and it is important for the scene that the actress show
Courage's belief in the war, did Brecht turn Ruth's suggestion
down.

When people asked me if Brecht was a hundred per cent
Communist, I used to answer, no, only ninety-nine but the
women in his life: a hundred and one per cent. It was Stalinist
Communism I was talking about. The actors who opened in the
Berlin *Mother Courage* as the Cook and the Chaplain left not
long thereafter for the West. Helene Weigel asked why. 'Well,'
explained one of them, 'it isn't very pleasant to be noticing how,
in the East, people – your colleagues sometimes – disappear one
day and are not seen again.' Weigel replied: '*Wo gehobelt wird,
da fallen Späne.*' – 'When you plane the wood, the shavings
fall.' 'It's just,' one of the actors rejoined, 'you fear that your
turn will come to be a shaving.'

When, in that autumn of 1950, Helene Weigel passed
through Munich and joined Brecht, Ruth Berlau and myself,
I had to feel that the Communists were in our midst, and I
was in the midst of Communists. Whether or not those three
conferred about Eric Bentley, I did receive an invitation from
Ruth that turned out not to have been entirely her own idea.
To dinner in the restaurant of her choice, and she chose a good
one. After dessert she got right to the point: 'Brecht wants me
to sound you out.' 'Something he couldn't tell me himself?' 'He
didn't want to overwhelm you. He knows you and I gossip
together and even know how to cuss each other out!' (This
was not Ruth's vocabulary. She spoke to me in German – with
her Danish accent. I answered in the same tongue – with my
Anglo-Saxon twang.)

'Why aren't you one of us?' 'Us?' 'Oh, you know what I
mean. I'm not afraid of the word! Communism! Or just anti-
fascism if you want to call it that! Why aren't you?' 'Well, I *am*
. . . sort of . . . partly . . . All my best friends . . .' 'Pah, we've
read your book! And don't you have a new piece saying Brecht
would be a better writer if he gave up Marxism?' 'Not exactly,
what I said was . . .' 'We know what you said. We are asking if
you are ever going to change!' 'Change?' 'Yes, change. Brecht
says, if all these rumours are true, and the Russians are about
to take over West Germany, it'll be very good for Bentley,

because they'll carry him off to Moscow and re-educate him. He'll learn a lot!' 'You're joking.' (I half-realized how black the humour was. In Russia I would all too soon have gone the way of Tretyakov and Carola Neher.) 'Oh, no, I have a very important message for you.' (She took a deep breath and leaned across the table.) 'Brecht is tremendously impressed with you. Thankful, too. He knows what you have done for him in America. So much. It's wonderful. You *represent* him there. But that's the question. Do you? Can you? On the aesthetic plane, yes, but don't you know what Brecht's aesthetic is? You do. But you "disagree" with it. That's what's wrong. Doubly wrong since Brecht is, well, *anti*-aesthetic! Content before form, you understand? If you're anti-fascist, progressive . . . why aren't you consistent . . . why don't you follow through?' 'Well, Ruth, where to begin? One of my close friends, Arnold Kettle, before I even met Brecht, was a Communist. Arnold and I argued all the time . . .' 'About what? What couldn't he satisfy you on?' 'Oh, the usual stuff – the Moscow Trials . . .'

I did not know at the time that Brecht was supposed to have said of those who were condemned in the Moscow Trials of the late 1930s: 'The more innocent they are, the more they deserved to die.'[5] But I did learn then and there that I had cited a crucial, perhaps *the* crucial, issue, for Ruth at once blew up. Literally *stood* up in the restaurant and shouted: '*Du bist so dumm* – you are so dumb! Ignorant too! What do *you* know about the Moscow Trials?' 'Well, I did look into them. And I didn't think they were on the level!' 'That's it, then. I have to tell you this: you can *never* represent Brecht in America while you represent reactionary views, while you are . . . on the other side in the fight!'

Neighbouring guests in the restaurant had turned to look at the shouting Dane, but the latter sat down quietly, paid the bill, and became entirely polite again. I thought maybe the incident hadn't happened. We were both a little drunk after all. Or that it wasn't serious.

Ruth never referred back to this conversation, nor did Brecht ever mention it. But, alas, it had happened, and it was serious, and, except for the swearing, Ruth meant every word of it, and did speak for her master, whether or not he had told her to handle it just as she did.

'And don't you have a new piece saying Brecht would be a better writer if he gave up Marxism?' So they knew about the *Theatre Arts* piece, and Brecht must have thereupon decided that my 'unpolitical' position wasn't as harmless or as unpolitical as he'd supposed. Perhaps I would come into the Communist movement just in order to be Brechtian Number One in America? An offer had been made to me. Was it an offer I could not refuse?

Hardly. For though, at this distance in time, I cannot measure the magnitude of my desire to be important in Brecht circles, to be his exclusive or near-exclusive translator, editor, and so on, I did know Brecht had misjudged the political difference between us. I don't mean I was at the opposite end of the political spectrum. *That* he could have handled. When not too busy explaining that they were really Nazis, he had a soft spot for reactionaries, business men, men of power, enemies you had to respect. He preferred dealing with them rather than with liberals and non-Stalinist radicals – with a very few exceptions in this last category, such as Karl Korsch. Just as a fanatic Protestant hates a Catholic more than a Buddhist or a Hindu, so Communists of the Stalin era loathed the Social Democrat more than the reactionary. Now my own politics had been wobbly. I had wobbled all the way over from absolute pacifism to an excessive enthusiasm for the Allied war effort, headed as it was by Marshal Stalin. But the only party I'd ever been in was the Independent Labour Party. That was in my Oxford days of the 1930s. It represented the kind of socialist I was and have been ever since: Social Democratic, not Communist.

Though I did not enjoy being named, later, as an Enemy by Helene Weigel, I would at any time have heartily accepted the word Opponent. Not of course in every respect. I can direct *A Man's a Man* and feel complete sympathy with what I conceive it to be saying. And so it is with many of BB's works. But on socialism there was always the deep disagreement. Perhaps I had been too quiet about this in the beginning from fear that Brecht would never let me get to know him if he realized how much of his thinking I rejected. Later on, he would find out; did find out; and declared the disagreement unacceptable. I must either agree to agree or . . .?

During Brecht's lifetime, I was not actually thrown into outer darkness, though I often felt I might be. I had to assume that Ruth reported our fateful conversation to her master but he never followed through by telling me I could not represent him in America or that he considered me reactionary and 'on the other side in the fight'. He had let me manage many of his American affairs before 1950 and he continued to do so afterwards. When an American, in this period, wrote him

65

about rights to a play, he referred him to me, saying I knew more about his affairs in America than he did himself. He continued to assign me various production and publication rights until his death, and a letter to me of 1954 shows that Brecht continued to regard me as politically salvageable (i.e. convertible to Communism):

> About your critical abilities, everyone agrees, except perhaps for a few blockheads, even if a few non-blockheads deplore your appalling lack of political education . . . Let me make a suggestion. I have put together a Collective for dramaturgy. The participants – a period of one to two years is envisaged – draw an income from the Academy . . . and have access to the Berlin Ensemble . . .

Which was exactly continuous with what he had written me shortly before our Munich crisis:

> . . . don't let yourself get bitter about my hesitation in having you direct plays in the commercial theatre . . . I would prefer that you should practise first in our theatre. If you see any chance of this, I would do much to help.

It was not until his heirs took over that I was definitely placed on the enemies' list. Clifford Odets and Charles Laughton were, of course, already on it. And it was not long before the three of us were joined by the very person originally chosen to denounce me: Ruth Berlau. Though dead, she is still being denounced in the 1980s by the Winifred Wagner of East Berlin's Bayreuth, Barbara Brecht.

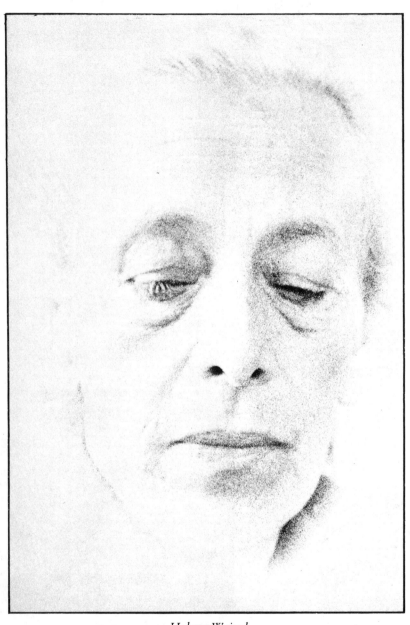

Helene Weigel
(photo: Inca Vilander)

Helene Weigel,
lithograph by Arno Mohr

Elisabeth Hauptmann

15

Chausseestrasse 125, East Berlin, June 1956. At an Ibsen celebration in Oslo, the Norwegian capital, I have got to know the chief drama critic of East Germany, Fritz Erpenbeck, who, from his days of exile in Moscow earlier, had defined a position on Brecht which at first blush looks much like my own: Brecht is a great writer, but one need not embrace his theory of an Epic Theatre. In Oslo, I have defended Ibsen the individualist against Brecht the collectivist. I am not aware that Brecht has been becoming more critical of Stalin in his last years or that he has been in close touch with the young Wolfgang Harich, leader of the dissidents among Berlin Communists. Actually, I have heard Brecht speak of Stalin's 'greatness' even after our fracas of 1950. I am not sure that I want to go to East Berlin to see him.

But of course I go. (Is that the meaning, perhaps, of the whole story I'm trying to tell?) I go: 'pünktlich wie immer'. Stalinism was indeed deeply troubling. (To Brecht also but I didn't know that yet.) But fundamentally I was never an *ism* person, and, though Bertolt Brecht professed to be an *ism* person, one might say *the* ism person, what I had felt was that really he wasn't. Or that he wasn't in relation to me.

I got a shock. Brecht presented himself as soon as he knew I was there. A physically shrunken Brecht. A Brecht who had lost his looks. (In his own way, severe, gaunt, a little haughty, Sphinx-like, he had been goodlooking.) Shrunken in the body, swollen somewhat in the face, flaccid. And without that familiar and so distinctive voice. What voice he still had kept sinking to a hoarse whisper. Gallantly – and he did have his own gallantry, had no self-pity that I could ever descry – he bade me welcome back to Berlin. I hope I didn't show signs of shock; but he assumed I *would* show such signs and said his health had not been 'too good'; he was '*etwas reduziert*', 'in reduced circumstances'. I told him the commonplace thing: that I was very, very glad to see him again. And he saw the reality behind the commonplace. Being a dramatist ('the most original dramatist now writing') he could read a subtext any time. Seeing my eyes, he also felt my vibrations. He knew all.

BB arranged for me to see three new or newish productions: *Trumpets and Drums, Playboy of the Western World,* and *The Caucasian Chalk Circle.* As usual at the Ensemble, I was much impressed every time. Each time it was theatre with a dimension more than theatre, even good theatre, as I had known it in other countries, and as I had just been 'covering' it for several years as dramatic critic of *The New Republic* in America. What was that extra dimension? Communism? – tell it to *The Daily Worker*! Walter Kerr, then with the *Herald Tribune,* had written in 1953 that Brecht speaks only to Bentley, and Bentley speaks only to God. Myself, I didn't feel that close to Godhead, certainly I had my less supernatural readers, albeit not as many as Walter Kerr, and I tried, with whatever unsuccess, to convey to them the impression that, initially Brecht on the printed page, later Brecht on the stage of the Berlin Ensemble, made on me. If I failed, it was my failure, not his.

After the three evenings in his theatre, a talk with Brecht in his apartment at 125 Chausseestrasse. (The 'arrangement' was now that Weigel and Brecht lived in the same house but on different floors, each with a bell at street level. Ruth Berlau had her own place within walking distance. She could pride herself it favoured Brecht's special preferences – not just his cigars but the kind of chair he liked, and so on – but actually she had lost him in his last years, not to Weigel, but to the younger generation, girls such as Wolfgang Harich's wife Isot Kilian. Ruth was drinking herself to death.) Brecht wanted to know my impressions of the three shows I'd seen. Were standards being kept up? Was anything wrong? Or lacking? Well, I said, *The Playboy of the Western World* was *all* wrong, beginning with the East Berlin interpretation of the word 'Western' as meaning non-Communist (what American politicians call the free world). That was laughable. And from it came a ridiculous interpretation of the playboy himself as a would-be Hitler. J. M. Synge had never thought of anything like that, so why should they, pirating his work, as I gathered they had? (It was still protected by copyright.) Oddly enough, in the twilight of his days, it was Brecht who was the easy-going worldling and I who was the zealot. 'Oh, well,' he shrugged, 'what else could we make of the play in this benighted land? We couldn't possibly reproduce the Irishness and the wonderful humour.' 'Then why do it at all?' I asked harshly.

The subject had to change. I had loved *Trumpets and Drums*, and thought that any historical-geographical errors in it were irrelevant. I held no brief for Farquhar's *Recruiting Officer* on which it was based, and saw no reason why it should not be fooled around with when the fooling was in such excellent taste and in so effectively light a vein. You can't be pretentious if you are pretending to nothing! The show had high style. Another re-discovery of art for art's sake? Good in any terms, the production seemed to me especially salutary in the East where the critical emphasis had been all too heavily on content as against form, message as against manner. On this BB could emphatically agree with grins and many nods of the head. Ever since the 1930s, he reminded me, he had tried to make the pundits of the East see that, while he agreed with them on message and content, *this was no reason to neglect form*. What's wrong with form? He knew he didn't have to explain this to me! Was I not his formalist friend? (He could disown me when I went too far. Very well. This too was a living arrangement.)

By this time, Brecht was longing to talk about his own masterpiece, which I had translated, *The Caucasian Chalk Circle*. Had the production let me down in any way? Or? No, no, I answered, I had had the time of my life. It was the greatest modern theatre in my life since *Mother Courage* in 1949. I had basked in its glory. Pick holes here and there? Perhaps. The Dessau music was so hard on the singers, one couldn't always make out the words, and wouldn't one maybe have welcomed music more conventionally tuneful? 'You sound like *our* critics now', says Brecht, referring to the disapproval of all musical modernism in East Berlin. I reminded him of my 'sympathy' with Erpenbeck despite the abyss between us. 'Extremes meet, huh?' says he, mischievously.

'Now let me ask *you* something,' say I, 'was Ernst Busch as Azdak exactly what you had in mind?' 'He's a great actor. He's my actor too,' says Brecht, 'but no. There was a dimension missing this time.' 'Ah?' 'Yes, he missed the whole tragic side of the role.' I was so fascinated by this comment, I had no comeback. Bertolt Brecht favouring tragedy? Finding in this comic, realistic role a 'whole tragic side'? A tragic side is not what East Berlin wished to hear about when words like renegade and traitor came so much cheaper! In Brecht's mind, when he wrote the role of Azdak, must have been Ignazio Silone and Arthur Koestler and their disenchantment with Communist revolutionism. *And is not that the kind of thing Azdak is all about*? I had noticed a book open and face downwards on Brecht's desk, it was Koestler's account of his Communist phase and what followed . . .

During all this I was alone with BB except that Frau Hauptmann kept coming in and going out for no apparent reason. Was she keeping an eye on us? Taking note when she heard things that shouldn't have been said by either of us? I thought of the culminating scene in Brecht's *Galileo* where the scientist's former student visits the great man for the last time. Galileo's daughter is now his jailer, and views the visitor with suspicion. Frau Hauptmann seemed worried that Brecht might hand me something he shouldn't by way of a remark or a joke. She would correct him now and then. For instance, he had a lot of fun with a Louis Armstrong record that someone had sent him, on which Satchmo sang 'Mack the Knife'. The lyrics were thrown to the winds, and Louis Armstrong was singing the familiar tune to any syllables that fit, such as 'Lou-is Armstrong, Lot-te Len-ya . . .' Frau Hauptmann didn't want me going to America to announce that this was acceptable to East Berlin! 'Decadent!' said she, 'American colonialism!' *'Aber doch,'* said BB, 'still and all, *das ist ein Neger*, that is a Black.'

Since I arrived in Berlin – city of rumours – I had caught the rumour that Brecht had been writing subversive stuff, even on Topic A: Joseph Stalin. Five years earlier there had been a large portrait of J. S. on Helene Weigel's wall. It was gone now. (Destroyed, I wondered, or relegated to the cellar against the day when J. S. might be rehabilitated?) If only I were the former student in *Galileo*, and he that great man, he would now pass to me a copy of his anti-Stalinist writings, and I would smuggle them out of East Berlin under the very nose of the watchful Frau Hauptmann.

Mere fantasy: Brecht's little 'Stalin (i.e. anti-Stalin) poems'[6] were to be totally secret for years to come, and indeed were semi-secret till they were officially published in 1982. If Brecht had daring thoughts, he didn't usually dare to make them known. Osip Mandelstam wrote a Stalin epigram, read it to friends, was exposed, and didn't live very long after that. Mandelstam's epigram called Stalin's moustaches 'huge laughing cockroaches'. They were still huge laughing cockroaches when Brecht made an imitation of them, sporting it on his own upper lip, and was photographed as Stalin. The difference is that the photograph, taken in the 1940s, was not shown around till 1978.

Brecht must have known that what I wanted to talk about was that 20th C. P. Congress in Moscow at which Khrushchev

72

had recently 'told all' about Stalin, but I did not force the issue, and he seemed to be steering me away from such matters of state. He wanted to talk theatre. So this is what I get for being the aesthete and formalist of the family', I was thinking. Brecht was saying: 'Helli thinks Ethel Merman would be the best American Mother Courage. Could we get her?' 'Alan Schneider has written us saying he wants to direct the play but with Helen Hayes in the part. Could she hack it?' 'They tell me it would be easier to arrange an American visit for the Ensemble if Walter Kerr came over and reviewed our shows. Can we get him to come.' 'Tell me about *My Fair Lady*. Is it something we could put on with our Regine Lutz as Eliza?'

As for my own plans in New York, what had happened to the Leo Kerz production of *A Man's a Man*? He (Brecht) had wanted the play put on during the Korean War: it would have had a lesson in it for America. And Howard Da Silva's interest in *Chalk Circle*? Had that too come to nothing? I laid my current project before BB: I wanted the rights to *The Good Woman of Setzuan* for Uta Hagen, Herbert Berghof, and myself. With these in hand, we would offer the play to his old and trusted producer, Hambleton. Frau Hauptmann was listening hard. Brecht nodded and said, '*Gut, die Hauptmann* will put it in writing.'

On my mind throughout was that I was looking my last on Bertolt Brecht. As for him, he was well aware of his condition, but there was nothing to do with the scene except underplay it. Büchner, not Schiller. 'Thank you so much for coming. Write me from New York.' 'Definitely. I trust you'll be fully recovered very soon.'

16

Truro, Massachusetts, 16 August 1956. Would Hambleton take the play? And us three with it? With his partner Norris Houghton, he came to my summer place on Cape Cod to tell me yes. I was already writing the English lyrics at a small reed organ I'd purchased for the purpose in the Wellfleet antique shop: I still have it. The day was 16 August. On that same day – melodrama à la Chaplin but flatly true – I received a cable from Johannes R. Becher, Minister of Culture in the German Democratic Republic, inviting me to a memorial meeting in East Berlin. Bertolt Brecht had died of heart failure.

I didn't go to Germany: told myself I couldn't afford it. I think now I just didn't want to face 'those people'; anyhow, contented myself with a return cable expressing sympathy.

Charles Laughton had also received 'the cable'. It fluttered his Hollywood dovecot. He called his lawyer: what should he do? The lawyer called the FBI and reported CABLE RECEIVED FROM RED COUNTRY. The FBI expressed its satisfaction at being informed and consulted, and gave a green light for Charles, also, to send a cable expressing sympathy.

I wrote the obituary that appeared in *The New Republic*, 27 August. Writing today (1985) I might use different language here and there: I do not sympathize with today's anti-Communists, nor accept the world view now called anti-Communism, but I am still anti-Communist in the simple sense of being against what passes for Communism in Russia:

BERTOLT BRECHT (1898-1956)

If at this moment I could write impersonally of Brecht I would say we have just lost our leading dramatist, but this is a man who has played a large, perhaps inordinate, part in my own life, and I am oppressed with the dull pain and inarticulateness that follows the death of a friend. And since the pain is mine, not his, anything I do manage to say is likely to sound outrageously egocentric. But it is this or nothing.

We were not intimate in the sense that we ever spent even months constantly in each other's company, and it is likely that he did not feel as intimate with me as I did with him. However, after the long periods of not meeting, I always felt welcomed back as a member of the family. The last of these reunions took place just two months ago. Brecht had had a heart attack in the spring, and was in Berlin just for a doctor's appointment. He kindly snatched an hour out of the trip for a talk with me. I can see him now rising from his chair, despite his weakness, and with all the correct, very German and bourgeois graciousness that was essentially his to shake me by the hand. We talked of this and that – of Louis Armstrong singing the Moritat, of *My Fair Lady* as a possibility for his Ensemble – and I can never forget that when I told him how Shaw's plays were being edited and cut now that he was dead Brecht said: 'One must never die.' His voice was gone as a result of the illness, but the old, Confucian smile still played around the set, thin lips.

He was a Communist, and I am anti-Communist, but I do not think people on my side have understood him very well. In theory he often showed disrespect for individuals and individualists, yet I had the experience of being his political enemy and his personal friend, and I must record that the friendship was given precedence over the enmity. At the throne of grace, like many others of us he will have to plead Inconsistency.

At a banquet in Oslo last May I found myself seated next to some of the leading critics and academics of East Germany, and they had no trouble at all in explaining What is Wrong With Brecht from 'the Marxist viewpoint.' 'For one thing,' said one of them, a rival Communist playwright,[7] 'he thinks no one but him understands Marx' . . .

He liked individuals, and was himself highly individualistic. His depreciators have to explain what it was in him that could take hold of you even though you didn't agree with him and he supposedly valued agreement above all else. He was, in the strict sense, the most fascinating man I have ever met. There were times when I hated him, but there were no times when I did not love him.

ERIC BENTLEY

17

Lotte Lenya and the Aftermath. The relationship of Brecht with Weill lies outside the scope of this eye-witness account of the former since I never saw the two men together. I witnessed only the aftermath through an acquaintance with Lotte Lenya, but of course recall things Brecht would say about Weill. He was catty on that subject, not only hinting that he himself composed the best tunes, but indicating that Weill had gone wrong where BB had gone right in the handling of American exile. 'Pity Weill was born somewhere else,' he would say with a wicked grin, 'if the Americans didn't have a law against foreign-born presidents, he'd have made it.'

What I am calling the aftermath consisted of my becoming an Enemy of the Brecht heirs, and a great deal of time was consumed in epistolary dispute and litigation. We never got before a judge or a jury, though at one point I submitted a motion for Summary Judgment to Judge Frederick van Pelt Bryan, who said no, and at another point we would have gone before a judge the following day at 9 a.m., had not an out-of-court settlement been reached on the phone at 9 p.m. Both sides spent quite a lot of money on lawyers, and sometimes the results were ironic, as when I for the first time in Brecht-Bentley relations received a cheque in four figures (from the Lincoln Center production of *Chalk Circle*) and my lawyer asked as his fee exactly the amount I had earned . . .

Rather than re-hash all this shabby detail, which might well bore me as much as my readers, let me tell a story that suggests the coin had a reverse side to it.

When my relations with the Brecht coterie were good, my relations with Kurt Weill's entourage had been bad, a fact that reflects the tension that had existed between Brecht and Weill since 1930. I am shocked today to pick up correspondence from the 1950s that bears witness to hostility between me and Lotte Lenya. It was partly my fault. As critic for *The New Republic*, I had been excessively snotty about the 1954 opening of *Threepenny Opera*: there was sibling rivalry between me and the adapter, Marc Blitzstein. Not surprisingly Lotte Lenya wrote East Berlin of her preference of Blitzstein to Bentley, and so on and so forth.

Luckily she and I were both people who did not know how to bear a lasting grudge and a business correspondence we began to have in 1961 burgeoned into cordiality by 1964. After that (I find I have some seventeen letters from Lenya in my files) my admiration for Lenya's work proved to be not altogether one-sided, and when I sent her my Hanns Eisler record album (*Songs of Hanns Eisler*, Folkways, 1964) she wrote me a bubbly letter which I would blush to quote in full, though I cannot resist citing the crowning compliment: 'It's quite wonderful to hear all those songs, and you do them so well that I am afraid you might become a close competition to me.'[8]

Lotte Lenya in Brecht on Brecht, *New York 1960s (photo: Henry Grossman)*

Appendix

There are eleven letters here, eight of them to Brecht. Three dots indicate omissions. Only 3 and 10 are reprinted from a carbon copy retained by me. I did not usually make any carbon or other copies; indeed some of these communications are just hurriedly scribbled (or 'scribble'-typed) postcards. The letter (2) to Jay Laughlin came back to me, in xerox production, through the kindness of James Lyon. Letter 4 is taken from *The New York Times*. Letters 5 through 11 (except for 10) are all taken from indistinct photo-copies supplied by the Brecht Archive in East Berlin: where these are illegible, it is so noted in the text. Eccentricities and inconsistencies of abbreviation, capitalization etc. have been retained: these were highly informal communications, never intended (except for 3 and 4) for publication.

1. To Berthold Viertel, an undated letter obviously written in March or April, 1945. It reflects the disillusionment that had followed the enthusiasm of 1942-3. Even at that, it makes the same distinction between Brecht the Man (often outrageous) and Brecht the Artist (always gifted) which W. H. Auden used to make. The Schnitzler mentioned here is Heinrich, Arthur's son, who at the time was directing *Master Race* in California. The Roberts is one Ernest Roberts, producer of the *Master Race* in New York.

Dear Mr Viertel:

I'm sorry my resentment against Brecht seemed to get transferred to you. . . .

I am not angry with you; but with Brecht I am, so much so that I regret having translated his play at all; it was a service he does nothing to deserve. For a couple of years I have been Brecht's only staunch supporter in the American liberal and literary press. I have spent much of my time and not a little small cash in trying to get his play produced. The result is that I now receive a wire from one person telling me that another person says that Brecht is consulting his lawyers about my actions. Meanwhile Brecht declines to reply to all my communications. He has been told about the Roberts affair and about everything else that concerns his play. But he has neither good manners nor elementary decency. He lives out his own theory that it is impossible to behave well in this society.

But for Schnitzler and Roberts I would wash my hands of the whole thing at once. However, these two men are working on the play, and I shall not tell them to desist unless Brecht himself writes to me and gives a full explanation of his conduct. It is his fault that both Schnitzler and Roberts are already involved; he knew about both projects from the start; and he did not write to me to stop them. Schnitzler's production is already in rehearsal. Roberts has been kept hanging around for weeks. Personally I do not see that S's production can be cancelled at all; and Roberts can only be repudiated if Brecht wants to act very unscrupulously – as a man like him, I suppose, does.

I believe I have stage rights, and not merely book rights, to the play, but of course I shall not use these rights. Brecht can consult his lawyers; I shall not consult mine (I don't have any). No. I shall do what Brecht wants, if he will only tell me *what* he wants, and tell me himself. When this is over, I wash my hands of Brecht. I shall apologize to Roberts if his production is cancelled, pleading that Brecht is an irresponsible and dishonest man. I shall not be interested in my rights to the play; in fact I think I shall sell them; I would like *not* to be connected with people of this sort.

Now let me apologize to you again for implicating you in the affair. I will be happy to help you with your article [on BB] if you will yourself negotiate directly with the KR [*Kenyon Review*] first. Nothing is altered between *us*. Nor does my opinion of Brecht's art change. He is like Dubedat in *The Doctor's Dilemma* – a scoundrel but an artist. All the best

Eric Bentley

2. To James Laughlin, New Directions' publisher, 28 February 1946. My correspondence with Laughlin had begun, I believe, with a letter of 17 August 1943, beginning: 'As perhaps you know I am interested in Bert Brecht . . .' It goes on: 'Mr Brecht . . . is very unbusinesslike, so I venture to write to you on my own responsibility. One of the mss. [sent me by Brecht] is quite definitely among the best work [sic] of recent times . . . This is FURCHT UND ELEND . . .' Later items in the correspondence with Laughlin find me furious with Brecht, as in the foregoing letter to Viertel.

. . . Brecht has now signed a contract with R & H [Reynal and Hitchcock]. He suggests me as his general editor but upon impossible terms. I'm to do all the dirty work and Brecht is to boss everything. Unless he withdraws his demand to supervise the whole show I must be counted out. I've had enough of Brecht and his female followers. He even asks that my introduction contain no criticism of his work! . . .

3. Internal evidence indicates that this undated letter was written in August 1946.

Dear Brecht:
 I gather from your letter [dated just August 1946 and quoted in *The Brecht Commentaries*, p. 288] that you do not today think of Epic Theatre as the one and only theatre of the future. In your Notes to the *Threepenny Opera*, however, you wrote: 'Today . . . only the Epic form can enable the dramatist to find a comprehensive image of the world.' Have you changed your mind?
 This question is not malicious; nor am I merely curious to learn the history of your mind. I am a little puzzled by your reasoning. Have you really explained the difference between Ibsen and Shakespeare for instance? Is it really true that the poet of *Peer Gynt, Ghosts,* and *When We Dead Awaken* is monotonous? Is it true that his forms are rigid? And even if it were so, would a comparison with the Elizabethan Age explain it? After all many of the Elizabethans wrote very woodenly. Or am I missing your point?
 I think I understand you and agree with you when you write: 'The very diverse theatrical forms are by no means attempts to arrive at a final form; only the diversity itself should be final.' But what are you saying about Bacon? Could you elaborate your distinction between Experimentalism as something provisional and Experimentalism as something much more important and lasting? You are right in thinking that it is too easy for people, especially for historians and critics like myself, to assume that our own age is purely an Age of Transition while certain other times were ages of fulfilment. The present is of course pure transition from past to future, and the present age *must* always seem purely transitional; fulfilment on the other hand is something that can be recognized only after the event. All this is true. Nevertheless not all ages are equally great, and one is bound to have some opinion of the greatness or un-greatness of one's period. My own impression is that the generation 1880-1920 was a much more fruitful one than that of 1920-1945.
 To you as a creative artist this may not of course be important. You will do your work and let others decide how good it is at their pleasure. You are indifferent to my historical and critical judgments for yet another reason: you are not only an artist but a teacher, a fighter, a 'propagandist'. You have a conception of art which few understand. I think I am probably

not one of the few. You will have to explain yourself. The explanation you gave in 'Telling the truth: five difficulties' was not enough. I felt that you brushed aside all modern art except your own kind. You brushed it aside; you did not really cope with it. I would welcome two things: a brief account of your philosophy of art and – but this can wait a little – an acount of Epic Theatre that deals with some of the difficulties raised by Edmund Fuller some years ago and, more recently, by myself (*The Playwright as Thinker*, pp. 259-61).[9]

These are troublesome demands. But I think you will do yourself a service if you can help American readers and playgoers to see the difference between 'Brechtism' and the impossible vulgarities of 'proletarian literature' of which the most impossible is Socialist Realism. Like Shaw you are more eager to explain your politics and your morality than your art. This is your privilege. But I warn you that you will never make any further advance in America unless you can dispel the illusions and doubts that at present surround your kind of enterprise. They will not listen to your message until they are 'sold' on your art. Yours ever

Eric Bentley

4. To *The New York Times*, 10 November 1947. The part of the letter they did not print – they themselves used asterisks to indicate an omission – is lost. Reference is to the Hollywood production of *Galileo*, evidently compared by a *New York Times* correspondent to Barrie Stavis' *Lamp at Midnight*.

ADVOCATES BRECHT PLAY
To the Drama Editor:

I do not know the play which your correspondent prefers to Brecht's. But I have just seen Brecht's play on the stage, which your correspondent apparently has not. I shall not compare it with Shakespeare or call in the aid of Miss [Margaret] Webster, but I shall say this: that it is unwise to condemn Brecht's play before you have seen it performed, and that in my opinion Charles Laughton's production of it constitutes the big theatrical event of this decade. Mr Laughton did not choose the play merely as a vehicle for his talents – though that would be a good enough reason if one considers what Mr Laughton's talents really are. He chose it out of admiration for the play as a play and as an important statement about science and social ethics. I saw his performance in Los Angeles three times. It is an astonishingly beautiful and instructive thing, and something different in kind from even the best thing one sees on Broadway.***

Eric Bentley
Minneapolis, Minn.[10]

5. *An undated postcard apparently sent from Salzburg to East Berlin in late 1949.*

Dear Brecht: I want you to read Erich Auerbach's *Mimesis*, published by Francke in Zurich. It is the best history of the idea of Realism that I know, much profounder than [Georg] Lukács.

In the background of the idea Verfremdung would you say the work of [Theodor] Lipps or [Wilhelm] Worringer was important? They elaborated the conception of *Einfuehlung*, which is, in a way, your starting point. I am interested in finding the broader setting of your dramaturgy.

By the way, one of the parts of the ORGANON I like best is the part on [illegible word or words] the Gestus. This is at the same time original and classical. You started out as an anti-Aristotelian critic. But the ORGANON champions 2 great Aristotelian notions: first, that pleasure is the end of art as of life and, second, that the heart of drama is plot.

People say: 'But after all Stanislavsky cannot be held responsible for all the excesses of his followers. And he didn't have a System: he had an Approach useful in all styles.' Question: what in Stanislavsky's books is useful for Narrative Realism (my name for Epic Theatre)? yrs E.B.

6. A postcard to Brecht's secretary Ilse Kasprowiak with address American Express, Paris, dated 18 October – the year has to be 1949. The present book being no place for business correspondence, the business-y part of the message is omitted.

. . . Eine Frage für Brecht. In dem Teil des ORGANONS wo er Hamlet resümiert, sagt er, dass Hamlet umkehrt, als er Fortinbras sieht und beneidet. Das ist nicht wahr. Er kehrt viel später um und aus anderen Gründen. Auch schlachtet er nicht seine Mutter usw. WAS MEINT DER BRECHT? Ich frage, der englischen Uebersetzung wegen. Es wird schwierig sein, diese Resümierungen von Shakespeare in Shakespeares England zu drucken. Oder habe ich nicht recht verstanden? Ihr – Bentley

. . . A question for Brecht. In that part of the ORGANUM where he provides a resumé of Hamlet he says Hamlet turns around when he sees and envies Fortinbras. This is not true. He returns later and for other reasons. Nor does he slaughter his mother etc. WHAT DOES BRECHT MEAN? I ask because of the English translation [of the ORGANUM]. It will be difficult to print these summaries of Shakespeare in Shakespeare's England. Or have I got it wrong? Your Bentley.

7. A letter from EB in Salzburg to BB in Berlin, prefaced by a message to BB's secretary: 'I must write in English because I have to explain some complicated matters. You'll see that Brecht reads this? . . .' Again 1949, the date is given as 12-15 November.

Liebes Fraülein: Ich muss auf Englisch schreiben, weil ich schwierige Sachen zu erklären habe. Sie werden sehen, dass der Brecht dies liest? . . . viele Grüsse, EB

Dear Brecht: I'll see that your revision [of the *Hamlet* passage in his *Organum*] and your footnote are used in the English version. Not that I am quite happy about the footnote – but it's your affair. I'm not happy about it because it introduces a principle not explained in the text: the idea that you can *change* the play and make it definitely different from Shakespeare's. Carry out this idea, and you'll have a *Hamlet* as different from Shakespeare as the *Dreigroschenoper* is from *Beggar's Opera*. I have no objection to such re-creations – provided that the result is NOT called an interpretation of Shakespeare. Interpretation and adaptation are in principle different things. You seem to me to blur over this distinction.

Your ironic remark about the golden West is doubtless justified as far as the West is concerned, but are you never ironical about the East? The fate of men like [Theodor] Plivier and Lukács is of interest, surely.

I bring this up because I have read your play *Tage der Commune*. [Kurt] Hirschfeld [Dramaturg at the Schauspielhaus, Zurich] says it's meant to refer to Berlin under the blockade, the Soviet blockade. And yet your play shows a city attacked only by capitalism. Is the analogy very exact? If Western troops are in Berlin and are engaged in a struggle, the struggle is with Russia and not with Germany. I see no equivalent to this in your 1871 situation. Or rather: to accept yr version of the story one has to accept the Marxist interpretation of 1871 in its entirety and one has also to accept the Russian interpretation of 1949, i.e., one has to think that the Communists in the East zone stand for rule of the Germans by the Germans in the fullest and sincerest way. Can you *really* believe this? [A couple of paragraphs that follow are very indistinct but the following statements can be made out:]

I don't know whether this letter will estrange you. Since you don't write anyway, the estrangement cd not perhaps, for practical purposes, be more complete than it already is. But I want you clearly to understand that I write as a proven admirer of yr work, as one who has been called in the *New York Times* a 'Brecht Disciple'. I do not think *Tage der Commune* is a good play. Considered stylistically it is made up of imitations of yr own earlier work. It seems to be lacking in all freshness and spontaneity. A big disappointment. [The prospect of E.B.'s directing *Setzuan* at the Oxford playhouse is then mentioned.] Of course I cd choose a play by someone more friendly to a Westerner like myself, but I still have an admiration for yr best work, an admiration that will survive our disputes or even our friendship. [The signature is just 'Yrs E.B.' after the news is given that 12 university productions of BB have been arranged by EB in America.]

8. This letter is dated 18 November and the year must again be 1949. It is almost complete. Above a Salzburg address is written: 'I hope you now have my article MODERN GERMAN STAGECRAFT? I wish you'd send any criticisms. It's in the KENYON REVIEW which I mailed to you. Something for Neue Rundschau?'

Dear Brecht: It was a great pleasure to have your letter [dated 12 November 1949, quoted in *The Brecht Commentaries*, p. 293] and to learn that no damage was done. I would indeed like to work with you in the theatre before proceeding to direct your plays myself. The difficulty is a practical one: I would have to know exactly *when* and *where*. As things are, I could scarcely accept employment at the Deutsches Theater even if you wanted to offer it to me. But when is your next production? It is possible that I could arrange to be present at most of the rehearsals. However, I need to know very soon.

My present plans are to be in Italy during December, and in January [1950] to produce *Setzuan* at the Oxford Playhouse, England. I take it I have your permission to undertake such a production as this . . .

I am directing a month of theatre for advanced theatre students in June 1950 at this Schloss [Leopoldskron]. Could you come? For a week? Or a couple of days? We would give you an official invitation which might facilitate your entry into Austria . . . A visit from you would be very important to me. I have been able to do much more for you here than at Minnesota, because the students here come from many different countries and take home what I say to various communities. A French translation of *Puntila* has already come about in this way. An Italian version of *Galileo* will be made. My production in England will be another pioneer job.

I doubt if you are right in suspecting that my gifts lie more in the theoretical than the practical direction – it is simply that you *know* more of my theoretical work. My temperament seems to me to lead more to directing than to writing. I would gladly be a director who also writes (not a writer who also directs). But I can't say that America seems to offer me the chance I need.

However, you must have realized that I am too little in sympathy with the present-day Communist parties, as led by Russia, to go over into the other camp just because they are more interested in theatre. I agree with very many of your criticisms of the West, but I think that the East is even worse. In West Germany it is true that ex-Nazis are getting encouragement, but what about the Deutsches Theater? This morning I bought a book by [Herbert] Ihering[12] published a few years ago. In it I find a clear and unambiguous endorsement of Hitler and even a picture of [Emil] Jannings 'in the liberated city of Danzig, October 1939'.

I think it quite possible that the Communists will throw you overboard one day, as they are rumoured to have thrown over Lukács in the past months and so many others in the past years. From their point of view you are indeed a 'formalist' etc etc: even [Erwin] Piscator, whom I talked to in New York [summer, 1949], levels this charge at you. But perhaps I am irritating you now?

As to your Hamlet question, what you say in yr letter seems more moderate and I think it is acceptable. I'll think about it again. [A half legible signature follows an illegible message and greeting.]

9. This must be 1950. The letter is dated simply 1 July, and again is going from Salzburg to East Berlin.

Dear Brecht: The well-known Italian manager and director Luchino Visconti wants to know if I could direct PUNTILA for him in Italy and in Italian during the coming season. It would be a full-scale production with the best actors. His season of theatre will probably be the outstanding event of the next two years as far as Italian drama is concerned. Naturally I am very eager to do this job, and since I saw *Puntila* in Zurich and Munich, and also discussed it with you in Berlin, I feel I could do you justice. At present my intention is to return to America in September but if you will approve Visconti's proposal I shall try to arrange to come and study with you during September and October . . . Since the planning of my whole future depends on decisive action now I hope you will help me

. . . Very sincerely, Eric Bentley

10. In Italy 1950-51 I experienced a small triumph and a less small setback. The triumph was my production of *The Exception and the Rule* with the Teatro Universitario di Padova, headed by Gianfranco De Bosio, a production that ended up gloriously at the National Festival in Bologna. The setback was the collapse of the Visconti plan for me to do a first class production of *Puntila* in Rome with Paolo Stoppa as Puntila. I sued Stoppa for non-payment of what he owed; and won; but this was Italy, and my lawyer took all the winnings: all! Letter Ten belongs to 1951 and is dated 27 January. It went from Padua to East Berlin.

Lieber Brecht: hier sind die zwei wichtigsten Artikeln über meine Brecht-Aufführung in Padua. Sehr intelligent sind sie nicht, günstig sind sie schon . . . Auch die Fehler dieser Artikeln sind symptomatisch . . . Zum Beispiel, der eine Kritiker schreibt, dass Altruismus der Beweggrund des Kulis war.

Die Première war ein grosser Abend. Ausverkauft – 1200 Zuschauer. Ein freches Publikum und zum Teil ein unwissendes. Die Musik von Dessau war 'fischiata' (?deutsch: verpfiffen). Auch die pantomimischen Teile, die ich zusammen mit einem französischen 'Expert' [Jacques Lecoq] gemacht hatte. Aber jemehr der eine Teil des Publikums sich ärgerte, desto mehr wurde der andere begeistert. Am Ende: Beifall, Beifall, Beifall. Die Musik, muss ich sagen, ist sehr schön, and wir haben fast die ganze Partitur gespielt. (In der Pariser Aufführung, wurden nur zwei Stücke davon gespielt.) . . . Auf der Bühne, benützte ich das Rundhorizont der COURAGE. Es war wunderbar für die ganze Reise des Kaufmanns – mit der Dessauer Musik and den Pantomimen des Lecoq . . .

Die Aufführung ist bei weitem meine grösste praktische Errungenschaft im Theater. Es ist das erste Mal, dass ich (ungefähr) zufrieden mit meiner Arbeit bin. (Da ist auch viel, was ich gerne ändern möchte – aber das sind Sachen, für die man Geld braucht: ohne Geld kann man einen grossen Realismus nicht schaffen!) Eine Brechtsche Aufführung. In München lernte ich sehr viel.

Die ganze Stadt Padua redet davon . . . Zaiotti, der Chef des Festivals von Venedig, war hier. Die Vorstellung hat ihm gefallen . . . Wann kann ich eine englisch-sprachige Aufführung [von *Ausnahme*] leiten? Fahre jetzt nach Rom. *Puntila* soll in März stattfinden . . . Viele Grüsse

[EB]

Dear Brecht, Here are the two most important articles about my Brecht production in Padua. They're not very intelligent but anyway they are favourable . . . Even the errors in these articles are symptomatic . . . For example, one critic writes that the Coolie's motive was altruism.

The premiere was a great evening. Sold out – 1200 spectators. The audience aggressive and in part ignorant. Dessau's music was *fischiata* (whistled at). So were the pantomimic parts which I created in collaboration with a French expert [Jacques Lecoq]. But the more one part of the audience got mad, the more the others waxed enthusiastic. At the end: applause, applause, applause. The music, I must say, is very fine, and we played almost all of the score. (In the Paris production, only two bits of it were played.) . . . On the stage, I used the cyclorama of MOTHER COURAGE. It worked wonderfully for the Merchant's whole journey along with the Dessau music and Lecoq's pantomimes . . .

The production is by far my greatest practical achievement in the theatre. It is the first time that I've been (more or less) satisfied with my work. (There's also a lot I'd like to change, but these are things one needs money for: without money one cannot create a grand realism!) A Brechtian production. In Munich I learnt a great deal.

All Padua is talking about it . . . Zaiotti, head of the Venice Festival, was here. He liked the production . . . When can I direct an English-language production [of *The Exception*]? Now on to Rome. Puntila should be on by March . . . Best wishes, (EB)

11. 1951: this letter went from Rome to East Berlin, 21 February.

Lieber Brecht: eine Katastrophe ist geschehen. Das Theater hat entschieden, PUNTILA in dieser Spielzeit nicht zu machen. Und das Angebot, das Stück auf Oktober zu verschieben, hat wahrscheinlich nur den Zweck, mich jetzt nicht bezahlen zu müssen.

Eine Schweinerei. Aber Sie wissen wie das Theater ist? Das Theater in Italian ist alles von kleinen Gangsters organisiert. Die wussten, dass ich den Winter in Europa passiert habe, um diese Regie zu machen. Und ich glaube, sie wussten schon in Dezember, es wäre unmöglich PUNTILA zu machen, haben aber nichts gesagt. Es war sehr 'convenient' mich da zu haben, falls sie keinen Erfolg mit *Death of a Salesman* haben würden. Aber sie haben Erfolg gehabt. Leider. Jetzt sagen sie, sie haben die Schauspieler für PUNTILA nicht . . . aber Sie können sich vorstellen, was für Diskussionen wir gehabt haben – Sie kennen ja den Broadway, also es ist dasselbe – Schwindel, Heuchelei, man wird Verrückt, weil niemand sagt, was er meint, alle sagen andere Dinge, und aus Diskussion wird 'shadow boxing.'

. . . Arbeitslos bin ich also. Mein Versuch ein Regisseur zu werden klappt nicht . . . Andererseits, mit dem was ich gemacht habe, war ich verhältnismässig zufrieden. Mir und dem Publikum habe ich gezeigt, dass ich wirklich ein Regisseur bin. Ich bekam soeben die Presse von Genova – über AUSNAHME UND REGEL. Ein grosser Erfolg. Die grösste Zeitung sagte sehr schöne Dinge von Ihnen und fand die Regie 'stupenda' . . . Alles gute, Ihr alter E.B.

Dear Brecht: a catastrophe has happened. The theatre has decided not to do PUNTILA this season. And the proposal to postpone it till October probably has the sole aim of not having to pay me.

A bad business. But you know how it is in theatre? In Italy, the theatre is run by small-time gangsters. They knew I spent the winter in Europe in order to direct this show. And I think they knew as early as December that it wouldn't be possible to do PUNTILA. But they said nothing. It was very convenient to have me on hand, in case they had no success with *Death of a Salesman*. But it's a success, alas. Now they say they don't have the actors for PUNTILA . . . but you can imagine what our discussions have been like – you know Broadway, and this is the same – swindling, hypocrisy. You go crazy because no one says what he means. They all say something quite different, and discussion becomes shadow boxing.

. . . So I'm unemployed. My attempt to make it as a stage director has not clicked . . . On the other hand, I was relatively happy with what I did. I showed myself and the public that I really am a director. I just got the reviews from Genoa – of EXCEPTION AND RULE [which was on tour]. A big success. The largest newspaper said very fine things about you and found the direction *stupenda*. All the best, Your old EB.

Notes

[1] I performed the speaker's part in Schoenberg's setting of Byron's *Ode to Napoleon*, and we sent a disc-recording made with very primitive equipment to Schoenberg. The latter wrote Jalowetz in somewhat imperfect English (letter dated 8 September 1943):

> As soon as I had opened the package I played the records. Let me tell you at first that what you have achieved in training Mr Bentley and in accompanying this difficult piece is so excellent that it gives me again an opportunity of beeing [sic] proud about my pupils. It is really a pleasure to see how superior all of them are to everything which figures as masters in our present time. I have no idea what Mr Bentley's voice is like. From the records no such sonority emerges which shows whether this voice has the compass (as to pitch) and the number of shades essential to express one hundred and seventy kinds of sarcasm, hatred, ridicule, derision, contempt, condemnation, etc, which I tried to portray in my music. It is also not to see whether the voice possesses the dynamic scale necessary to all that. But especially it is impossible to find out whether the voice has the 'euphony' without which a success of the recitator with the snobbish New York audience would be impossible. On the other hand I was astonished how well everything was done as regards rhythm and declamation. I consider this as very excellent and if, in New York, they find a good answer to the problems beforementioned, I would say that Mr Bentley would be qualified for this performance . . .

[2] But in some cases explicable. My friend James K. Lyon was allowed to see certain material *on condition that* he say little or nothing about Brecht's offspring. When he asked me if I thought he was wrong to accept such a condition, I answered, No, not if he told his readers about it. However (in *Bertolt Brecht in America*) he did not tell his readers about it.

96

[3]This fact is borne out by the edition in print in America in 1988. The word Realism crept back in – carefully defined, I trust – in some earlier editions.

[4]Hardly a common expression in English, it is all too common in German, and its use in the third act of Berg's *Lulu* was the reason why Arnold Schoenberg refused to help finish the orchestration of that opera.

[5]The report that Brecht said this in 1935 was not made till 1960. In *The New Leader*, 30 December 1968, I gave reasons for not taking such a report too seriously. The reporter, Sidney Hook, angrily exclaimed that I was impugning his veracity. I had only meant to suggest that memory – certainly in twenty-five years – plays strange tricks. But Henry M. Pachter wrote in to the magazine to aver that, in thus daring to differ with Mr Hook, I was insolent (*The New Leader*, 28 April 1969).

[6]The most outspoken of them runs as follows: 'the czar spoke to them/with gun and whip/on Bloody Sunday. then/there spoke to them with gun and whip/every day of the week, every work day/the honoured murderer of the people./the sun of the peoples burned its worshippers./the most learned man in the world/forgot the communist manifesto./the most gifted student of Lenin/punched him in the puss./when young he was conscientious/when old he was cruel/young/he was not god/who becomes god/becomes dumb.'

[7]Hedda Zinner, not-so-incidentally wife of Erpenbeck.

[8]I did ask permission to print two of Lenya's letters in full but Lenya's executors refused. It seemed they didn't wish the public to find out what she thought of Stefan Brecht.

[9]Edmund Fuller criticized Brecht in *One Act Play Magazine*, April 1938.

[10]In lieu of the lost passage, let me supply this excerpt from a letter to my editor Harry Ford, dated 12 August 1947: 'We drove down to Los Angeles to see the Brecht *Galileo* which was really magnificent. I still don't think the play great, but the ensemble of play and production is very fine. Laughton's

performance is very brilliant and also – which is more remarkable – very solid. The production is the first satisfactory Brecht yet seen in America . . . The whole affair was very encouraging and fascinating . . .'

[11]Revision and footnote were provided in a letter from BB to EB dated 31 October 1949. They were incorporated in the English version included in Toby Cole's *Playwrights on Playwriting* but, as far as I know, nowhere else.

[12]Ihering, the first important critic to recognize BB's gifts in the early 1920s was, in the late 1940s, working at the Deutsches Theater.

The playwright Heiner Müller and Eric Bentley – parricides both?
Brecht's daughter Barbara has described Müller as 'der Vatermörder'.
When he was introduced to Bentley, he exclaimed, 'Der andere
Vatermörder!'
(photo: Schandorff)

Eric Bentley in the 1980s
(photo: Stethis Orphanos)

Postscript

I still think I was right to keep myself in the background of the first edition of this little book. After all, it was to be a memoir of Brecht, not autobiography. At the same time I was uneasy when friendly readers found me mysterious and when less friendly readers found me evasive and/or disingenuous. Reading the memoir now, I see that my determination to be self-effacing left holes in my narrative and perhaps prevented the reader from learning what I was up to.

What I feel might be misleading, when I read the memoir now, is the detached tone. Brecht is on stage playing to the hilt the roles I assign him, striding, gesticulating, at times even screaming. I am the quiet spectator/reporter. Not that I (often) wasn't. Not that he didn't scream. I was the interviewer; he, the interviewed. He expected it to be that way and was used to getting it that way. He was creating his own image in the minds of his admirer, and why not? Who was I to feel insulted at receiving no comparable attentions in return? But when I hear people remark that he concealed so much from me, I can only retort that this 'so much' was as nothing beside what I hid from him. Even in the Memoir above, I admit withholding differences of opinion, lest they break up the relationship we did have. But the real withholding was that of my soul – spirit, if you prefer – both when we first met and later when he assumed he knew me pretty well.

Most of the readers of the Memoir, probably already had some idea who Brecht was and knew by what strange turns of fate this deeply German writer had come to be living in the neighbourhood of Forest Lawn and Aimée Semple MacPherson's Temple when World War II was at its height. What they could not be asked to guess, were the equally strange turns that brought me there. His starting point was Augsburg, Bavaria. Mine was Bolton, Lancashire. I come of what a snobbish brother of mine called sturdy yeoman stock. My paternal grandfather put us on the path Up-From-Wage-Slavery. From being a simple mover of furniture, he acquired a horse and van and created Joseph Bentley, Bolton, Limited, Removal Contractors. Inheriting this business with his brother, my Uncle Frank, my father acquired first, a second horse, then a steam van, and later the motor vans which were to be seen in that part of Lancashire for some decades. In short, my family was enacting the same drama as millions of other families of the Western World in this era: the drama of upward mobility from the depths of poverty to the dizzy heights of the lower middle class. After I had left for America, my father would be mayor of the town.

My mother was equally interested in the journey to gentility but what she gave me in earliest childhood was far more intense than social ambition. It was faith: religious faith, implicit, unquestioned, ardent, total. We were Baptists and devout churchgoers, Sunday School goers, too. My mother's idea of a normal Sunday was church in the morning, Sunday School in the afternoon, and church again in the evening.

I say my mother *gave* me faith. I should say rather that she strove mightily to give me faith and that at first she was successful. Only this would explain the fact that the fullest experience of happiness I've had in my more than seventy years was the moment each night when Mother would come to my bedside to hear me say my prayers. What is bliss? Negatively defined, it is absence of qualm or anxiety. Positively, it is a delight in blending, merging with Mother, with Nature, with God.

She was fully successful at first and intermittently successful for some years thereafter. After that, bliss became a will o'the wisp, not always recognized as such. What had intervened? Non-faith. Doubt. Unbelief. Where does *that* come from? I have no memory of it but Mother told me later that when she first told me, in outline, the life story of Jesus, I said, Is that true, or is it a legend? Her reaction, she said, was amazement that I knew the word *legend*. Even if I was only four, I had already had at least one experience that created radical doubt. At three, two lumps, like two small eggs, swelled up on my neck. A doctor, I was told, would come and remove them. I was in my baby chair (operations were performed at home in those days) when this man approached me, razor in hand. Doubtless, it was a scalpel, but what I was familiar with was my father's open-blade razor. He had a large black moustache with wax tips, like Kaiser Billy. I had a clear image of what was happening: a Giant was coming to cut me up. I screamed. My mother was present, after all, and standing just behind the

Giant: her job was to save me. I can see her clasped hands now, and the anxiety in her face, but she made no move. The world belonged to the Giant, and the Giant, advancing, said to the now terror-struck me: Be a man.

I realize that persons who ask (among other malign questions), What causes homosexuality? and who, in any case, love to attribute any uncongenial human traits to traumas of infancy, will now pounce. Be it so. The Gestalt of this little scene was burned into my consciousness and my unconsciousness: oneself as infant in the baby chair, the all powerful male Giant-with-the-knife poised for the fatal blow and, in the background, the mourning mother, either helpless or will-less, but doing nothing, accepting impotence as her role.

A small child who fastens on a grown-up word like *legend* will be congratulated on his brilliance but what he has actually done is intuit that one day he may sorely need the word, and more than half a century later I would have to write a play called *From the Memoirs of Pontius Pilate* in which I separated the legendary Jesus from the historical. As for belief and unbelief, the second had been added to the first but had not replaced it. I oscillated painfully between the two forever after. Later, I found the phenomenon encapsulated in a single sentence of Kierkegaard's: 'We are double in ourselves, so that what we believe we disbelieve and cannot rid ourselves of that which we condemn.' It is a principle that articulates itself in a myriad ways, as I realized when a friend told this story about me. He had ridden the subways of Berlin with me after the city was divided in two in 1949. He said that, when the train was in the Western stations, I made heads turn around by aggressively worded anti-Western remarks, but that, as the train made its way to the first East Berlin station, my position changed so blatantly to an anti-Communist one that, really, I should take care or I might be arrested. My first reaction when I heard this story was to feel flattered: it sounded like the story of an effectively Socratic gadfly. But when I let my mind dwell on it, I could only remember the torment that had always attended my feeling for the truth of A when I was openly espousing the truth of B, its opposite.

At puberty, the young Baptist is asked if, unlike those Christians who are baptized without their permission in infancy, he is going to be baptized into the faith. For my part, I loved my mother, and I loved Jesus (or what I took for him), and I said yes. I was baptized by total immersion in what resembled a small swimming pool just below the pulpit of Claremont Baptist Church on Saint George's Road. I had high expectations of the big moment. (Also low expectations, disbelieving what I believed.) I liked the minister, was even prepared to have a bit of a crush on him. But when he held me in his arms, and lowered my head into the water, I came up chilly and dripping and learning that wet clothes cancel out romance, even romance with God. It was not long before I told the minister I had difficulty believing. In reply he sent me a religious greeting-card with this sentence from John's gospel: 'Whosoever willeth to do His will shall know of the teaching, whether it be of God.' I read it many times and decided I understood it but had not found it to be true. I had after all willed to do His will when I expressed the wish to be baptized. But I did *not* know whether the teaching was 'of God'.

Nor was I ever to find out. Worse: the terms of the question were beginning to disintegrate when, in pursuit of education and gentility, I won a scholarship to Bolton School where the official religion, affirmed by hymns and prayers every morning, was not confirmed by the teachers who made the strongest impression, nor by the books they gave me to read. What does the word 'God' mean? What would it mean to know the 'will' of a God? But of course the spirit of contradiction works both ways, and even while the ideas of the Free Thinkers were seducing my adolescent spirit, the will to believe asserted itself, too, as vigorously as its opposite. If philosophy represents a pure will to know, while religion reflects the will to believe, then my nature was ever religious rather than philosophical. And when, later, I came to devote myself to the arts, the art that held a unique fascination for me was the art which since Greek days has itself been fascinated by beliefs: the art of the drama. I would learn that other kinds of drama have also been proposed, particularly in our day, with its drama of the bedroom and the front porch. When I was a professional dramatic critic, it was a foregone conclusion that my reviews of such plays would be negative.

In my undergraduate years – at Oxford where another scholarship in the same cause brought me – I was still not prepared to break with organized Christianity but I sought out its least organized, least theological institution: the Society of Friends. That was my negative reason for joining it. There was a positive reason: its pacifism. I was not yet of university age when Oxford students voted that they would never fight for King and Country but I was caught up in that surge of anti-war sentiment while still at Bolton Scool. One of my teachers knew

Robert Graves, and I read Graves's *Goodbye to All That* along with other already famous products of World War I like *Death of a Hero, Memoirs of a Fox Hunting Man*, and the poems of Wilfred Owen. It wasn't clear to me (still isn't) that the New Testament preached pacifism but it had a pacifist element, and guided by Tolstoy one could isolate and endorse this element. I was prepared, at the time, to be politically as simplistic as Tolstoy. The world seemed headed for a war that would destroy civilization but this could be prevented if enough people would refuse to take part. My will to believe, more and more detached from any theology, could lead me to believe in this.

Communism was the sophisticated thing, in the mid 1930s, for student rebels to believe in, but I was not sophisticated. I wasn't upper class enough for Oxford proletarianism. I felt that immediately on hearing Philip Toynbee make Communist speeches at the Oxford Union. How, without the right accent and self assurance, would one ever get into a club like that? Literary Communism appealed to me but only in a literary way. The plays of Auden and Isherwood were in the Communist orbit and opened up for me a vision of a lively new kind of theatre, especially if they had music by Benjamin Britten. But the odour that came off all these men was unmistakably Public School. Marxism was something (I thought) which they must have picked up on their expensive vacations on the Continent.

I don't know why I didn't feel the same way about Aldous Huxley whose *What Are You Going To Do About It?* I championed against C. Day Lewis, a future poet laureate, who at that time wrote a Communist riposte to Huxley under the title 'We aren't going to do nothing'. Huxley, too, belonged to the English upper class's argument with itself, but what he had to say about war reached many of the rest of us, even the most class conscious and suspicious. What he was writing in that period met my needs, and since the will to believe carries with it a will to act on one's beliefs, commit oneself to them, I, who had broken with churches, joined two pacifist organizations, The Peace Pledge Union, and the Oxford University Pacifist Association. I was the first Chairman of the latter, and in this period, for the only time in my life, I joined a political party, the Independent Labour Party.

What would happen if war broke out and neither civilization nor myself disappeared from the scene? It was a question I had to answer in 1939. But how could I? Initially I was able to float along on assumptions made earlier. As a pacifist, I would declare myself a conscientious objector and enter a camp for such. Indeed I was in a camp near Birmingham when news came that I had won the scholarship to Yale, which I had applied for the previous winter. Would the British government give me an exit permit? It did. After the blackout I'd left behind me in Birmingham, the neon lights around New York Harbour announcing WRIGLEY'S SPEARMINT were an astonishment. I had left the continent where everything had ended and come to one where nothing had begun.

But for me there began a new double life. Outwardly, it was business as usual, which for me meant continuing my studies, distinguishing myself. My life as a scholarship boy was a continuous success story from my entrance to Bolton School at eleven, to my entrance to University College, Oxford, at eighteen, my promotion to Senior Scholar at New College, Oxford, in 1938 and now a two-year term as Commonwealth Fellow in the USA. I had the choice between Harvard and Yale, and chose Yale because they would let me get the doctorate in less time. I now placed myself in competition with the intellectual athletes in America as I had already done in England. My friend Richard Ellmann, the famous biographer-to-be, won the Porter Prize for the best doctoral thesis of general human interest in 1942; I had won it the year before.

'Keeping up appearances' is usually spoken of slightingly, as if one's duty were to keep up no appearance and run naked, but looking back I'd say that a degree of professional proficiency and success was what preserved my sanity and kept me, most of the time, from thoughts of suicide.

1939 was not the first year in which my life had been in danger of total collapse. But the last time this had happened – when I was eleven – the crisis was overt: what doctors then diagnosed as 'nervous breakdown' was accompanied by high temperatures, fevers and chills, nightmares and hallucinations. The crisis of 1939 was both better and worse, better in that there were no visible or measurable symptoms, but worse in that their very absence left me facing, in full consciousness and good health, the fact that my world had blown away: I was no one and inhabited nowhere.

I don't know if anyone who did not live through the 1930s can imagine the state of mind of those who did. In addressing my own sons, I must say: *Since you will have illusions of your own, try to bear with us in ours.* Until September 1939, I thought any general war must destroy civilization (as today we presume that World War III would do). But when World

War II came and life for many of us continued, I discovered I had never really believed war would come at all. I had been näive enough to assume that the nations just would not do it. And one consequence of my näiveté was that I had in no way prepared my psyche for war, for any role in war, least of all the role of a war resister, which, for one of my class, can be a harder role than that of a soldier: in uniform I'd probably have been assigned to non-combat duties, out of uniform it was gaol or picking up broken bodies on the battlefield in an ambulance unit.

If my body escaped to America, my soul did not. *Coelum non animam mutant qui trans mare currunt.* If only I'd been running away from war to a country really at peace, life would have been simple and understandable. But I knew from the first that peace, for America, was precarious and could end any time. And what disturbed my spirit was not my unpreparedness for soldiering but unpreparedness for conscientious objection in war time. Pacifism had not been more to me, I was learning, than making sure war did not come. And my religious training had taught me not to cast oneself for a heroic role without the specific strengths it would require. A non-saint should not play at saintliness, nor non-heroes at heroism.

Well, the American Fellowship would be a reprieve, not a solution or a refuge. It would buy me time to find out where I stood. Perhaps I could coast a while longer on the formulae I had been living by in England? In New Haven, Connecticut, I looked up a Friends' Meeting House and attended a couple of Sunday services. They were not helpful. I learned that some Quakers were moving away from pacifism. And everyone present was American and still remote from war itself.

Had I miscalculated in coming to America? I could have stayed among the pacifists in England until it became intolerable, if it did, and then I could have joined the army with millions of others at that time. I really didn't know why I hadn't stayed home. With hindsight I suspect that the part of me that impelled me towards flight was not political. The 'home' I was fleeing was not the British Empire, it was 152 Markland Hill Lane in Bolton, Lancashire. It was a flight above all from my mother. Which will come as no great surprise to the few among my readers who knew her. She was a powerful Victorian matriarch. As a child I had worshipped her. As an early teenager, I had an intense crush on her. If I rebelled in my late teens, I was still in awe of her and fearful of incurring her displeasure. I knew she laid claim to infallibility in theology, so it was not easy to drop the Baptist faith when it meant dropping her. And at least as troubling as religion was sex.

My mother, a Yorkshire woman born in 1883, celebrated no wedding anniversaries because her eldest was born less than nine months after marriage. She had known nothing of sex then, and didn't learn much more later. As a young man I learned that she never knew how to exercise birth control. Babies just came. There were none after me. Just before I was born, my father had an accident, and was in Manchester Royal Infirmary for many months. No sex with his wife afterwards, I imagine. She had never liked it anyway, she gave me to understand. It was brutal, dirty, and you couldn't imagine Jesus doing it.

I don't know if she knew about homosexuals but when I was fifteen or so I had a big crush on a boy in my class at Bolton School and Mother went to consult the only woman teacher there. She was worried about us keeping company too much. We were not having sex. I had already played with other boys' genitals now and then, but I didn't connect those small events with the adoration I now felt for Derek. I would go to his home and instead of playing games or talking we would just lie together on the couch, touching but not carnally. I've seldom had more blissful hours than those, and they enable me to understand the 'Oriental' respect for absolute stillness and Walt Whitman's affirmation of sheer loitering.

The teacher told Mother that such things were common in boys' schools but that the boys got over it later, and I suppose that, since I got over Derek, or he me, Mother imagined the 'problem' had evaporated. The dualism characteristic of my life in general made my sexual experience and inexperience also ambiguous and contradictory. Although the flavour of the feeling for my own sex seemed to me as innocent and delicious as that of strawberries, I knew the horror in which it was held by persons of my mother's background and I developed a terror at the possibility of being found out – a continuation of the fear, verging on panic of having my masturbations found out. I gather that the liberated generations of today are no happier than we were, but surely they must be miserable for other reasons. For us the stigma of being found out would have been unbearable. But the strain of hiding was so great I had to run away, from Bolton, from Britain, whenever an opportunity offered, as in 1939 it did.

When I read the lives of upper-class homosexuals like Christopher Isherwood, I envy them. They had to pay attention to the taboos – Isherwood left the sex out of his early book accounts of his life, and Auden addressed love poems to lovers whose sex was unspecified – but they could arrange to live in 'gay circles' and have an abundant love life. Myself, even after I'd run away from home, and moved in the privileged circumstances of an Ivy League campus, I was too shy to hunt out the like-minded. After two years of Yale, I was still a virgin as far as women were concerned, and I had made a carnal connection with exactly one fellow student who, like myself, pretended to be straight. You may ask how, in that case, anything ever happened? Through fantasy. Scott and I, locked away in his college room, would indulge in sexy talk – heterosexy talk, after which discretion could be thrown to the winds. But when it was over, the talk would turn to anything but the topic before us. We never kissed, hugged, or, when parted, wrote love letters. Scott is long dead now, and I don't know if he ever turned out to be what he or I would regard as gay.

I didn't realize it then, but what I sorely needed in my love-life was what I needed in religion and politics: a belief to which I could be committed. In all areas I was now a hollow vessel, and I was on my own. I had abandoned one country without adopting another. I had less and less religion; politics were now a mere vestige of an era that had passed; no women, having rejected my mother and not having approached anyone else; no male lovers, except for a few minutes on a few occasions with Scott; no friends. I made several stabs at friendship and worked up a crush on someone clearly heterosexual, who never figured out my 'strange' behaviour. How I behaved towards Richard Ellman I cannot accurately remember. Evidently he thought I had made a pass at him, and delivered himself of a homophobic diatribe. Correction: I did make one real friend, Arnold Kettle. Arnold also picked up his Ph.D. at Yale, and went on to write two of the best volumes extant on the nineteenth and twentieth century English novel.

I wonder if MI5 knew whom the Commonwealth Fund was bringing to the USA as young ambassadors of imperial Britain? Of the small group, one (myself) was a pacifist who had, so to speak, stood on soap-boxes to declare that he would never fight for king and country; another had kept no secret at Cambridge earlier, and would keep no secret at Yale now, that he was a member of the Communist Party. Arnold was a conspicuous member of the Party in the UK until the 1970s. My qualms about my pacifism being still secret, in conversation I inevitably espoused the cause I'd belonged to in the 1930s, and there were some harsh exchanges in the early days. Later we learned to keep the talk out of the danger area. Arnold's temperament was propitiatory: it was gentle and flexible, and his sense of humour embraced all the shadings from subtle irony to a broad sense of the ridiculous. He was tolerant, too, and I remarked that this was strange in a Communist. 'No,' he said, 'you believe in tolerance because you're not tolerant; I don't because I am.'

Arnold and I were able to make common cause: neither of us supported the war or the prospect of America's entry into it. This meant we were making common cause also with people who appalled both of us. We even turned up one evening at an America First Rally on the Yale campus. The chief speaker was Colonel Charles A. Lindbergh, whose fear that Slavic hordes might be about to pour in through Alaska did not appeal to Arnold. However, he continued to abet the crowds who cried: The Yanks are not coming! until Hitler invaded the Soviet Union.

That event sent Arnold rushing back to the UK and into uniform. It made no difference to me. Or did it? I kept no diary or other record and can report only from the perspective of nearly half a century later. Spiritually, I endured a black night of the soul for all of two years at Yale, but this was a secret I shared with no one, no one I'd left behind in England, no one I had met in America. Arnold could only have supposed I stayed to avoid the war, a pacifist unwilling even to volunteer for ambulance service.

I was stuck. There was no turning back but I had no idea in which direction to move forward. Was there any movement at all by mid-1941? In order to write this Postscript I dug up the doctoral thesis I submitted to Yale in the spring of 1941, the one to which they gave a prize. Mostly, it is busy keeping up the appearances: I had learned to come on as the star student of the year. Intellectually, though, there *had* been movement since 1939. Although detachment from the war is announced as appropriate to the thinking writer, the ideas analysed and lingered over, are those I was not even acquainted with before the war. Fatalistically, I say that what is happening in our time is best exhibited in Alfred Rosenberg's book, *The Myth of the Twentieth Century*! The mind behind *my* mind throughout most of the manuscript is that of Friedrich Nietzsche.

Looking for the ideological roots of Nazism, I had become fascinated with the enemy. That was the meaning of my remark about Rosenberg. I addressed a letter to him, via his German publisher, to ask if I could translate parts of his book into English. I read other Nazi writers and a number of their forebears. But then I fell in love with the enemies of the enemy, beginning with Nietzsche and of course culminating, for me, in Brecht. Meanwhile I was living more and more among German refugees. I married one. It is no slight to that entrancing Austrian-Jewish girl that in marrying her I felt I was marrying into Central Europe. And I became very close to the Viennese poet Berthold Viertel, who belonged to the inner circle of Brechtians. Then it was Brecht himself.

This was later. But already in that 1941 thesis, it was clear that the näiveté of my pre-war pacifism was gone, and I was now approaching an abyss: belief in nothing. Though in the thesis I affirmed a belief in the intellectual who stands *au dessus de la mêlée*, even my negativism was ambiguous. Picking up the manuscript today, the first thing I notice is two epigraphs. One is a series of remarks by Heraclitus, along the lines of *War is the father of all*. The other is a quotation from *The Brothers Karamozov*, beginning with the Grand Inquisitor's words: 'We have taken the sword of Caesar and, in taking it, of course have rejected Thee and followed him.'

When I was cramming for my Finals at Oxford in 1938, I reached for a book to distract me for half an hour. The one book in my room that seemed to fill the bill was *Crime and Punishment*. I hadn't killed an old woman, but the tale drew me in as if I had. I didn't put the book down till I'd finished it. Now I had not only lost the vital hours that should have been given to cramming but found an author who spoke directly to me. Three years later, Dostoevsky made a second visitation, and this time it was *The Brothers Karamazov*. From it I tore the quotation that seemed to confirm the nihilism to which I was tending. What Dostoevsky was doing, both times, was interrupting my progress, reminding me of my Christian origin. For if I had rejected God, Jesus of Nazareth was someone I remembered and would continue to remember. If I had rejected Christianity, there is something, I now believe, which one can call the Christian spirit which is not to be rejected.

When Arnold sailed back to England to fight for the Empire and the Soviet Union, I asked the United States for a resident visa. I still felt I had nothing to offer either the army or any pacifist resistance, but something must turn up to fill the terrible void within me or I would cease to exist: I saw things in terms as simple as that.

It turned out that, though Arnold had not won me over to Communism, he had helped to make me more realistic about political power and more willing to accept, with whatever reservations, those centres of power which are the warring nation states. Had I felt that Russia was 'the future, and it works' I would have gone there. Having left my motherland, I was free to choose any country that would take me, and in 1939, the United States happened to be the country that offered me a Fellowship. But even before that I had been known to some, at Bolton School, as the American: I had played one in a production of Galsworthy's *The Little Man*. But it contained a germ of further truth. The Fellowship did not come out of thin air. I had asked previous Fellows what America was like and I did most deliberately choose New England as the best replacement for Old England. In 1941, even expecting something to turn up was a step forward.

At the same time I remained, and remain, European, and I surrendered the last vestige of my pacifism upon studying a very European document, *Man's Hope* by André Malraux. The book was written in the late 1930s when he was still in his quasi-Communist phase. But it wasn't Communism I got from the book. It was the feeling that one could no longer, in the world of Hitler and Franco, decline to meet force with force. My pacifism had been a tactic to avoid war. Once war raged, I could not, with Gandhi, advocate lying down in the path of the invading panzers. Whether or not I'd be assigned to combat duty I now felt I should offer myself to the armed forces. My first choice – a sort of irrational compromise between Britain and the United States was the Canadian Army. A Canadian Colonel interviewed me in Ottawa, following through with a letter in which he wrote: 'The projects on which your services might be used have not yet sufficiently crystallized . . . and I am unable to take advantage of your kind offer . . .'

Back in the States I had only to await the call, since, as a resident alien I was subject to the draft. The call came in December 1942. It was an anti-climax. At the induction centre in New York, clad in just my jockey shorts, I was confronted by a bespectacled psychiatrist in tie and three-piece dark suit. When he asked if I was attracted to persons of my own sex, I thought it would be odd, as well as mendacious, to say no, even though at the time I was engaged to be married. My reply, however, made him very nervous, and he quickly turned me over to uniformed officers. One of them was aggressive, eager to check out if I was lying to evade the draft. Where did I find partners? What exactly did I *do* with them? I thought he wanted to put me in gaol or a mental home but he handed me over to a colleague delegated to try the opposite approach, coaxing and suspiciously androgynous: he seemed to caress my shoulders while calling me Eric and asking if the sight of a good looking young man gave me an erection. I replied: 'not usually'. The androgyne put his arm round me and said in a melancholy voice, 'Well, I don't think the Army can use you at present', and I was released. I had however to be formally allowed through a military checkpoint where the clerk put a capital H against my name, while his friends, crowding around him to read his papers, cried: 'Homo, another Homo!' I was staggering uncertainly as I left the building and when I reached the sidewalk outside I had to lean on the wall for support. My attempt to join the war on political grounds had been coolly (or hotly) rejected by the war-makers on sexual grounds.

Arnold's persuasions did, belatedly, have some effect. When I took the United States for my country, I let myself be drawn into the now widespread enthusiasm for its ally the Soviet Union. Within a few months of the invasion of Russia, many of us were seeing a film called *Moscow Strikes Back* on Times Square. Little did we know that, in the Ukraine, Hitler's armies had been received with open arms. We took the word of Churchill and others that Marshall Stalin was in the forefront of resistance. 1942 to 1945 is the one period of my life when I knew what it was to be a Soviet sympathizer. My first translation published in book (booklet?) form was a tract called *The Thugs of Europe* written, probably under a pseudonym (I don't have a copy to consult), and without my name on it anywhere, by Albert Norden, a Party functionary later to be a prominent member of the East German Politburo. Did I know he was 'that kind of person' at the time? Well, once, when I was spouting the Party line in his small apartment on the West Side of New York, he shut me up fast, looking nervously over his shoulder: 'Sh! You don't have to convince *me*.' At least one commentator has concluded that in all this I showed myself a Brecht protégé. But when I met Brecht in the spring of 1942, it was because I was already in the Soviet camp. I was taken to Brecht by the movie director Herbert Kline, very much a fellow traveller except in the period of Stalin's pact with Hitler, as a sympathetic person to work with him.

Had I been moving in a contrary direction – say, towards the circle that wrote for Dwight McDonald's anti-war magazine *politics*, which I diligently read – no one would have offered to introduce me to Brecht, nor would I have wanted to be introduced.

Thus the young man whom Brecht met in the spring of 1942 was a political sympathizer, though far from being a Communist. As a sympathizer, he would often be *called* a Communist. 'You're a Communist!' Sidney Hook shouted into my face the first time we met, in 1944 or 1945 on Thompson Street in the apartment of Jeanne Wacker, who had been my student and disciple and was now his. Hook had himself been a sympathizer twelve years earlier and was still able to think along Communist lines: 'Objectively, Bentley's a Communist, just hear him talk about Russia.' But it was only the Russian war effort that appealed to the sympathizers of that time. We were not Marxists. We had no intention of joining the American Communist Party. My first book, *A Century of Hero Worship* – a re-write of my thesis – was reviewed by Hook in *The Nation*, and he noticed the Stalinist tendency of one passage in it. The *New Masses* (Communist) reviewer noticed it too, but where Hook was almost ready to cry: Communist! (something he likes to cry anyway) the Communist reviewer noted that I had, from his point of view, some distance to go.

As I said in the *Memoir*, Brecht did not seem particularly aware of my passing enthusiasm for the Soviet Union, so naturally he was not aware of the passing itself. In my political development, acceptance of power, even of what is now called super-power, was the first phase of my attempted self-reconstruction. After the disenchantment of 1939-42 came a certain excessive, even bumptious, fatuous enchantment with the world. That had to stop. And if a single individual had much to do with my Russophile phase (and this was Arnold Kettle, not Bertolt Brecht), a single individual had much to do with my ending it. This was Lionel Trilling.

I have led not just one type of double life but several. A double life I cultivated during World War II had these parts: I consorted with Brecht and his Communist associates; and at the same time I sought out scholars and critics in the academic world in which, after all, I made my living. (A fool has offered his guess that my motive in taking up Brecht was money. But the Brecht enterprise never helped me to make my living until after Brecht was dead.) My scholarly friends were never leftists. The first had been C. S. Lewis at Oxford. My relationship with him was delightfully dialectical. He would roar with merriment at my outrageous heresies. An unbeliever in his eyes, and beyond recall, I was accepted as a debating partner, a highly flattering role for the slightly precocious boy I was at the time. I learned a lot about Christianity from remarks of his that were above and beyond the call of duty, for he was only hired to teach me English Literature.

In America the two academics whose brains I wished to pick were Jacques Barzun and Lionel Trilling. I read their books, wrote them of my interest, and proposed that they serve as examiners at Black Mountain College, which was not allowed to provide examiners of its own. They agreed. I got to know them, and it was *their* non-Communist philosophy, not the Sidney Hook variety, that brought me into conflict with my commitment, albeit limited, to the ideas of Arnold Kettle and Bertolt Brecht.

From 1943 to 1945 I was a frequent contributor to *The Nation*, the liberal journal which Barzun, Trilling and Diana Trilling then wrote for. The magazine at that time led a double life somewhat as I did, politically speaking. The front-matter was in the Communist orbit, the back keenly if somewhat quietly anti–Communist. Given my tendency always to assert the A part of myself if my interlocutor was asserting the B part, it was inevitable that I would take the Communist side when dealing with the literary editor who was a fierce anti–Stalinist. That got me dropped from *The Nation*, as a sequence of events not dissimilar later got me dropped from *Partisan Review*. But this little bit of journalistic history is worth remembering after all this time only because it caused Lionel Trilling to give me a piece of his mind in several letters. The first of them ran to eleven pages.

This was in 1946, the year in which I set out my idea of Brecht's theatre in *The Playwright as Thinker*, the year in which he read the book and agreed to embark on a publishable correspondence about Epic Theatre and the like. Several years later, Brecht was to describe me as virtually the only champion of his theories. I mention this here to indicate the extent to which I lived in Brecht's world while, in Trilling's world, where also I lived, I was reading such words as these:

I live with a deep fear of Stalinism at my heart. A usual question at this point which I know you would never ask is: And not of Fascism? Yes, of Fascism too, but not so *deep* – in one's fantasies one can imagine going out to fight one's

Fascist enemies quite simply; but whenever I fantasy fighting an enemy that has taken all the great hopes and all the great slogans, that has recruited the people who have shared my background and culture and corrupted them, I feel sick. I am willing to say that I think of my intellectual life as a struggle, not energetic enough, against all the blindnesses and malign obfuscations of the Stalinoid mind of our time.

These remarks come from a rather bulky correspondence between Trilling and me that was prompted by my annoyance at Sidney Hook's review of *A Century of Hero Worship*. Trilling detached himself from Hook by stating that he knew I was not committed to Stalinism, but he went on to deplore that I would only go as far in the other direction as to cry: A plague on both your houses! As for Stalinist writers, none of them was any good. Brecht's work, he admitted, he did not know. Malraux's *Man's Hope* was a fraud.

The years following World War II find me moving far away from Stalin. In 1948 I became an American citizen, and I'm sure the Brecht circle took for granted that I supported their candidate for the American Presidency, Henry Wallace. My colleague F. O. Matthiessen, with whom I had a number of friendly talks that summer, was prominent in the Wallace campaign. I took no part in it and did not vote for their man. The tactic that I felt I had to adopt towards Brecht was that of quiet listening. But I was open in what I published. Mostly he never saw nor heard any of this. As reported in the Memoir, when he did hear something, there was trouble.

I can never forget the face or the vocal style of Wolfgang Harich, an East German intellectual last mentioned in the newspapers when he was gaoled for subversion in 1956. The face and voice I remember belong to 1949, when young Harich was Stalinism's latest convert in East Berlin. Lunching at Die Moewe (The Seagull), the élite artists' club, I was able to listen in on many conversations, as well as take part in a few. Clearest in memory is a tirade by Harich on the subject – a sensitive one for me, as I have explained – of Dostoevsky. Our friends in the West, he said, are surprised that Dostoevsky is not favoured in the Soviet Union. But how right the Russians are! This author must be totally banned. His works are REINES GIFT (pure poison). At which Harich's voice, already high and touched with hysteria, cracked ... Was this, for me, a third visitation? Surely Dostoevsky's ghost was whispering in my ear: Behold, the possessed!

I am offering these fragmentary notes on my political history to help trace the evolution of the author of the Memoir in the very years when he was seeing Bertolt Brecht. And what we find in the years 1942-46 is yet another duality. The zeal of the war effort, headed by Churchill, Stalin, and Roosevelt rescued me from philosophic nihilism and perhaps from absolute self-destruction. On the other hand, this zeal had itself a large corrupt component. By the time Brecht invited me to work at the Berlin Ensemble, in the 1950s, I realized that my listener's, learner's stance would entail a good deal of hypocrisy if I was to last out the proposed year in East Berlin. And by the time Brecht died, I was ready to describe myself in the obituary as an anti-Communist.

I had not become an integrated personality, free of contradictions. I had merely got rid of one particular set of illusions. During my last meeting with Brecht two months before his death, I continued to be a fairly silent partner, and never came near reporting to him the depth of my antipathy to the whole East Berlin enterprise. From the outset our relationship had been founded on misunderstandings, and if from time to time it changed, the change was from one misunderstanding to another. But when people find me arrogant in my studies of Brecht, I have to agree. The seemingly diffident observer, quietly concealing fundamental disagreement, did implicitly claim to understand Brecht's work better than those who agreed with him, or congratulated him on agreeing with them, in loud voices, a dogmatic tone, and an officially approved lingo.

I hope that this Postscript has filled the gap left by the Memoir, but it is possible that Bertrand Russell was right when he wrote, 'The things one says are all unsuccessful attempts to say something else.'

E.B.
New York, 1988

Index